a field guide to
NOW

notes on mindfulness and life in the
PRESENT TENSE

CHRISTINA ROSALIE

Guilford, Connecticut
An imprint of Globe Pequot Press

To buy books in quantity for corporate use
or incentives, call **(800) 962–0973**
or e-mail **premiums@GlobePequot.com.**

skirt!® is an attitude . . . spirited, independent, outspoken, serious, playful and irreverent, sometimes controversial, always passionate.

Text design: Sheryl Kober
Layout artist: Maggie Peterson
Project editor: Ellen Urban

Library of Congress Cataloging-in-Publication Data is available on file.

ISBN 978-0-7627-7856-0

Printed in China

10 9 8 7 6 5 4 3 2 1

For my father, who taught me to love the questions.

For Todd, who helps me to find the answers.

And for Liam and Rian, who teach me to love the process.

Contents

Introduction vi

At the Outset: Action x

In the Dark: Approach 6

Waking Up: Attention 14

In Between: Becoming 20

Close Like This: Bravery 30

Departure and Arrival: Conception 40

Nothing Lasts: Depth 48

Fight or Flight: Dialogue 54

In the Thick of Things: Discovery 62

Growing Pains: Fervor 70

Moving to Be Still: Habit 80

The Moment at Hand: Hunger 86

Lines and Sparks: Hurdle 94

Give-and-Take: Intersection 104

Off Track: Journey 112

At Home in the Moment: Listing 120

For the Time Being: Measure 130

Certain Uncertainty: Opportunity 142

Evidence: Prayer 150

Encountering Possibility: Prototype 156

Deciding: Timing 166

Taking Flight: Tyro 172

Acknowledgments 180

About the Author 181

Introduction

Every day is a journey, and the journey itself is home.
—Matsuo Basho

This is what I know: Remarkable things emerge from the smallest, most ordinary circumstances—from taking note and then taking action.

This book is in your hands because making it became unavoidable. Its inklings persisted, even when I was afraid, even when everything else in my life was riddled with uncertainty. Its truth showed up again and again with such insistence until I could no longer procrastinate, or pretend that there were other, more important things to do, or shrug it off with the promise of "someday." And so one February, in the same week as my sons' birthdays, I put myself 100 percent behind it and asked for support with an open heart. I launched the project on Kickstarter, and friends and family and complete strangers backed it. I cannot express how deeply grateful I am for the opportunity their support created. Their funding afforded me the possibility of taking the time to focus wholly on the work of creating, of turning the drafts and sketches scrawled in my notebook into something tangible and certain. It gave me the courage to claim this work for my life.

This book is evidence of that work. It is a glimpse into the turbulent process of becoming, and a reference manual for the observations, artifacts, and bits of wonderment that emerged from that process. It is both an invitation to you to create whatever opportunity your heart yearns for and proof that it is possible. To begin, to be in the mess, to be right here. Because it is in these ordinary moments—of writing lists, sharing things, keeping secrets, preparing food, sleeping, making love, fighting, rushing, folding laundry, and dreaming—that we become, always and again, whoever it is we are meant to become.

Each chapter has the following elements:

Essay: Containing the intimate, raw, and immediate stories that examine the fabric of the present tense. Arranged sequentially, the essays reveal a narrative thread from one entry to the next. It should be noted that this sequence is neither entirely chronological or linear, as the present tense is at once much bigger and messier and also smaller and more precise than the scope of such a timeline.

Field Notes: Alphabetically arranged for the sake of quick reference, these are the definitions, notes, and observations that I've found to be essential to the process of exploring the moment at hand.

Illustrations: Bookending each chapter, you'll find the front and back of a postcard, illustrated with the intent of sparking your unconscious and awakening curiosity about the emotional terrain and texture of the present as it applies to your own life.

Invitations: On the back of each postcard, you'll find an activity, question, or assignment that will help you to engage the varied circumstances of the moment as it applies to your life.

It is my hope that this book can be useful to you as a kind of survival guide, and also, possibly, an adventure guide for pursuing an authentic, passionate, creative life against the many odds of living with children underfoot, too little sleep, too little money, and never enough time.

The chapters are short, and there is breathing room in this book on purpose. It is meant to give you some space to pause, to wonder, to discover, and to create. You'll see. You'll find yourself here at the page, and then gone in an instant on your own adventure of identifying the moments that are unfolding in your life. You can read it straight through, or read starting anywhere—looking for inspiration or seeking clarification, the way you might use a field guide.

FIELD GUIDE

field guide | fēld gīd | (n.):
1. a guidebook designed to help the reader identify flora or fauna or other objects of natural occurrence; often containing illustrations and descriptions of characteristics and behaviors; 2. a manual generally designed to be brought into the field for identification purposes.

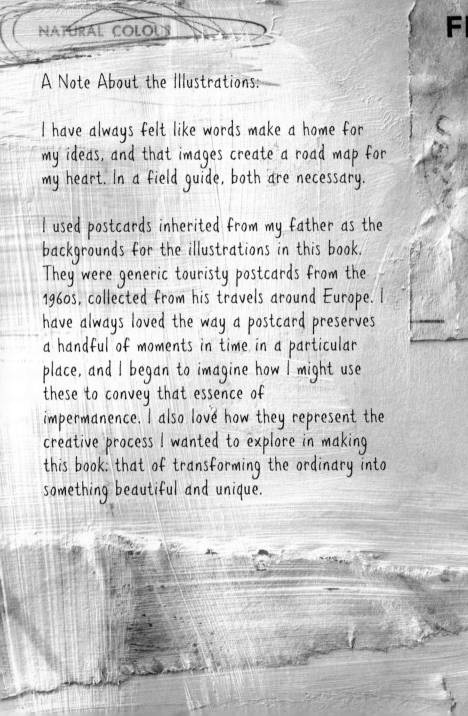

A Note About the Illustrations:

I have always felt like words make a home for my ideas, and that images create a road map for my heart. In a field guide, both are necessary.

I used postcards inherited from my father as the backgrounds for the illustrations in this book. They were generic touristy postcards from the 1960s, collected from his travels around Europe. I have always loved the way a postcard preserves a handful of moments in time in a particular place, and I began to imagine how I might use these to convey that essence of impermanence. I also love how they represent the creative process I wanted to explore in making this book: that of transforming the ordinary into something beautiful and unique.

At the Outset: Action

I am sitting, eyes closed, face upturned to the sun, when I feel compelled to look down at the grass beside me, and there it is: a frog, half inside a snake—its brief life already obsolete among the universe of small things that make up these woods, this sloping grassy hill, this place that I call home.

I've come to this spot much the way the snake must have, drawn by the sunshine falling in slanting angles onto the dying grass, and I can picture the way it might have been: uncoiled, its striped body lying like a forgotten hair ribbon on the ocher stubble of the lawn, its blood warming gradually in the weak October sun. Then the quick seconds when the frog approached and the snake pulled back its head and struck. A sudden silent struggle among the crumpled autumn leaves.

My three-year-old sees me watching and runs up the hill from where he's been playing near my husband, who is splitting wood. He launches into my lap, his questions eddying and eager.

I point to the snake.

His first reaction is to poke it, curious and unafraid. I hold him back, acutely aware of how the snake is captive here beside us in its process of devouring.

"Why is he eating that frog, Mama?" Liam asks, watching the snake's body expand and contract, its mouth gaping wide, wider as the frog's glistening belly slides slowly in.

"I guess he's hungry," I offer hopefully.

"But now the frog's not alive anymore, is it?" He looks up at me, his eyes reflecting the trees.

"No." I say this softly, hoping he'll just leave it at this, but of course he asks, "Why?"

The snake lies still now, its body as thin as the handle of a wooden spoon, save for a lump the size of my son's small fist, and I wonder if it is capable of movement at all. I wonder if it has any capacity to comprehend how perilous this moment really is. One quick swing of the spade, a fierce peck or two from our plucky rooster, or even the indelicate fingers of my small boy, curious and clutching too tight. I wonder what portion of its life span this moment is for the snake. For Liam these minutes still make up some easily calculable fraction of his life. But for me, the seconds keep on speeding up. The years tear by now, each one faster than the last, time rushing by my cheeks like a fierce wind.

How urgently I want something to hold, to be *for certain*.

I look up at the pale sky and think of how the stars above us are obscured by day. A hundred million suns like ours, their light already old, maybe even expired by the time it reaches us at night, twinkling like holes poked into the overturned colander of heaven. And without meaning to, I reach out to grip the grass, gravity suddenly improbable as I try to explain this small circumstance of living and whatever lies beyond.

"Because it's just the way things are," I murmur finally with the smallest shrug.

And then he nods and says "Oh," as if this is the most sensible explanation in the world, and scoots forward in my lap to get a better look.

To be alive means something different when you're small. Small children are only aware of the moment they are in. To them, life and death are only instances when certain stories begin—and maybe they are closer to the truth. Yet I'm five months pregnant with my second son, and more than ever now, things feel unsteady, every circumstance uncertain: the economy, my relationship with my husband, my work. More than ever I want to dash off and leave everything behind. I also know that it wouldn't change a thing. Survival and thriving are the poles between which the moments of life are strung. The balance is tenuous, and the outcome for each of us is different. Yet we mostly start with the same raw stuff: skin, a mother, shelter, breath, and each moment as it unfolds, one after the next, right now. Living with uncertainty is simply what it means to be alive, day after day.

Now when Liam looks up at my face, there is a clear trail of snot running down his upper lip.

"I'm gonna go see if I can find more snakes," he says slyly, squirming from my lap. He doesn't notice the way I've faltered, the way my answer is incomplete, or how my eyes are wet with sudden tears. Instead he leaps up and runs off down the hill away from me, his arms akimbo, his hair a mess in the wind.

I do this too much: Think of the future and miss the present. I get caught up in the uncertainty of things to come, instead of simply doing this: sit where I am, hold onto the grass, and notice what I can. As the sky fills with herringbone clouds and the snake finally slithers off in the dying autumn grass, I know what I must do: Take hold of the present, and begin to document the process of being right here, with the snake and the frog in the brittle autumn grass, and the heft and sweetness of my son in my lap.

I have no idea that what I am considering is the first inklings of what will become this book. I only know that I have a certain indescribable longing to keep some kind of record of the present as it unravels. I only know that I have the questions: What might it mean to be at the heart of the ordinary moments that make up my life? What might it look like to document the nuance and traits of this time as it unfolds, with my heart blooming in quiet wonder again and again as I arrive right here?

Field Notes:
ACTION

action | ˈak shən | (n.):
a gesture or movement; the process of doing something, typically to achieve an aim; to bring into effect a plan or idea.

I want you to know that this is the way things almost always begin: innocuous and small; a note jotted down on a napkin, a phrase that circles around in your head for days, a feeling you cannot ignore. This is when you must pay attention. This is when you must do whatever you can to begin. Let this book be an invitation.

Leap with arms flung wide toward the heart of your life.

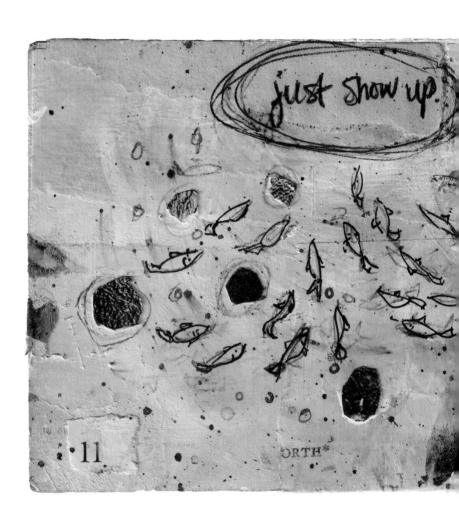

In the Dark: Approach

Outside in the cold a dog barks. Three sharp yips, then a pause, rain spitting against the windows before it barks again, punctuating my thoughts with irritation. In the sky the moon climbs higher up the edge of the dark, and inside on the couch I feel peripheral to my limbs and heavy belly, like a jellyfish that is present only in its own electric pulsing. I watch the slender steepled finger on the clock move into position at the twelve, the shorter one at the eight, and tiredness spreads through me like a slowly rising tide. I sink farther into the cushions, exhaustion making my legs at once jumpy and soft. The cat curls against my thigh and her purr is a metronome of comfort until I rub her fur the wrong way. Then she leaps up in a sudden aerial twist, lands softly on the floor, and struts off.

I should follow suit. Get up. Do things. I should wipe the counters, fold the basket of wrinkled sheets, and put the house back together after a day at work. But the clamoring of children still rings in my ears. "Teacher, teacher!" they chant all day. All day they want things from me: smiles, praise, attention, stories. And all day I give, until I begin to feel like a tap left to drip. Then I drive, probably faster than I should, to the day care where my son is waiting with stains on the front of his shirt, his arms held up to cling like a small marsupial tightly around my neck. I find his extra clothes and lunch box, tug on his boots, buckle him into the car seat, and navigate toward home.

When we arrive, the cupboard doors are askew. Jars sit like panhandlers on the counter, missing lids. The sink is full of dishes. My husband, with his lovely brown eyes, comes out of his office, distracted but beaming. He holds his arms open wide.

"Daddy!" Liam dashes to him.

We make dinner and then eat at the butcher-block counter. A fork falls to the floor, a glass of water spills, dinner dishes join the other dishes in the sink. Then there is tooth brushing, and stories, and the blurry eternity of lying beside Liam in the dark, singing softly until his eyelids close. Then I move like a slow robot, first one foot, then an arm, then a leg, until I am off the bed, across the room, and out the door. Tonight his eyes stay closed and I hold the banister and tiptoe down the stairs. Then I crumple here among the cushions.

My feet ache. My teeth ache. My ears ring. In my temples the vibrations of the day still hum. I feel worn thin like the fabric of a blanket too used, too loved, too folded and unfolded to meet the needs of other people's daily lives. So when the cat stalks off I feel like crying.

I might once have argued that depression only haunts those who have it hiding in their genes like varicose veins, the blueprint for sorrow already stamped onto the double helix of their life. But now I am beginning to understand that it's more like the mold that grows on the bread I leave in the pantry a day too long, or under the autumn pumpkins that sit, fat and secretive on the ledge while their bellies turn to rot. It's here in my life now, blue, and hazy, and obscure. It feels like frostbite. Something numb and slow, traveling from the peripheries toward the very center of my chest. It's the kind of ache you can't put your finger on or say, Here, do this, take that, and it will feel better.

Maybe it's this: Teaching children and having them has created some kind of stalemate in my heart. My days feel endlessly trivial, yet endlessly full. I end up doing one thing, to do the next, to do the thing after that, to end with bedtime. Only then does the small reel of my own life finally begin to unwind and play. Yet all of it is important. Everything I'm doing needs to be done. Nothing can wait or be dropped just yet. Each day there are test scores and meetings, and there is packing Liam something for lunch, and kissing his face, and saying good-bye, and then saying hello again. There are dishes, and benchmarks, and phone calls to return. And there are monthly doctor's appointments where I must get undressed and sit waiting with my growing belly in front of me like a pale harvest moon. I can see how it is possible to spend decades like this, just doing the day to be done with it, all the while waiting for children and incomes to be bigger, for time to slow down, for opportunity to arrive without effort.

Or maybe it's that winter is inevitable and soon. I keep saying it's that. I keep saying it's because the daylight is dwindling and the temperature has really started to fall. I feel unprepared for winter's length and dark. Already it is becoming an ordeal to get outdoors. Hats and gloves are necessary now, and mittens for the little one, which he hates. Boots too have become a struggle as the baby shifts under my ribs when I bend down, and my breath has to go somewhere and so I exhale, and exhale. I am still waiting to feel like I can inhale again. Yellow leaves flutter like clouds of paper beneath our feet when we go for a walk, and in the morning there is filmy ice on every puddle, like the skin that forms on milk left out all day in a cup on the counter, though bubbles still rise when I poke my booted toe in, and I know that even with more time and longer days, with blossoms and waist-high grass, this thing will continue to numbly spread if left unchecked.

So I begin.

I hoist myself up from the couch, pull on boots and a jacket, and then lean in at my husband's office door.

He still has charts up from the day on his various monitors: white screens with jagged lines and black screens with colored numbers that move steadily, though the market's been closed for hours. He doesn't look up until I say, "I'm heading out; need anything?"

"Why?" He swivels around partway to look at me now, an eyebrow raised. It's a fifteen-minute drive to the nearest open store at this time of night.

"We need milk," I say with a shrug. Because we do.

"Can't think of anything" he says, turning back to his screens. "Drive carefully."

The air has that bittersweet fragrance of autumn, of late grapes drying on the vine, and wood smoke and wet leaves. I can see my breath already. Above me, the bare crowns of the trees tuck up the night sky like a quilt pinpricked by stars.

I find what I am looking for under fluorescent lights in the aisle alongside glue sticks, wrapping paper, Post-its, tissues, and tape: a

$1.79 steno notebook that flips vertically, with yellow pages and a thin red line down the middle. I pay for it along with the milk and some dark chocolate, and when I get home, I set the alarm clock for 5:30 a.m. with a kind of fierce conviction I have almost forgotten I am capable of.

In the morning I will wake up and write. I will do it reluctantly. I will do it with urgency. I will do it because I know what it can provide. Writing in the morning is something I've done often in my life. It's a practice that requires everything and almost nothing—a cheap notebook and the commitment to show up and see what the page offers, first thing. The difference is that this time I'm turning to it as a lifeline.

It's the most obvious thing in the world once it occurs to me, but even obvious things become invisible when we look past them for too long. I've been so focused on keeping my head down, my feet going, one in front of the other, that I've forgotten that I can write myself out of this mess. I am someone who needs creative purpose with the same urgency that I need air, and it's this that I've let dissolve like sugar in the torrent of need rushing at me. But if I can wake up and write daily until I feel like I have a reason to be writing again, then I can write myself a raft. I can write oars. I can write buoyant water.

The moments might not offer themselves up to you the way that you expect. Maybe 5:30 is blue and dark and your sleep is too important to get up then. Maybe your days are already too long, and your dream time too short. This is okay. This is, in fact, what defining a creative practice is all about, especially during times when things feel dark, or bleak, or terribly out of focus. This work is about taking note of what your moments are made of. What they offer, and what they resist.

I start by writing in the morning, but gradually my practice becomes about carrying my notebook everywhere again. It becomes about paying attention to the little things and allowing them to fill the whole page, eclipsing worry and distraction: the chip at the scalloped edge of the white dinner plate I use for runny eggs; the way the sky fills with pale gray clouds that promise snow; or the crows, black and garrulous, that alight on the tree beside me at the intersection as I wait for the light to change.

Whatever it is, make your practice something that can bear some revision. Revise it, and revise it again, until it becomes something that truly sustains you—ten minutes every morning with quick brushstrokes, maybe, or pages scribbled in a notebook that travels with you everywhere. Let it be small. Let it be honest.

Field Notes:
APPROACH

approach | ə'prōch | (v.):
to move toward something;
to set about, undertake, or
embark on.

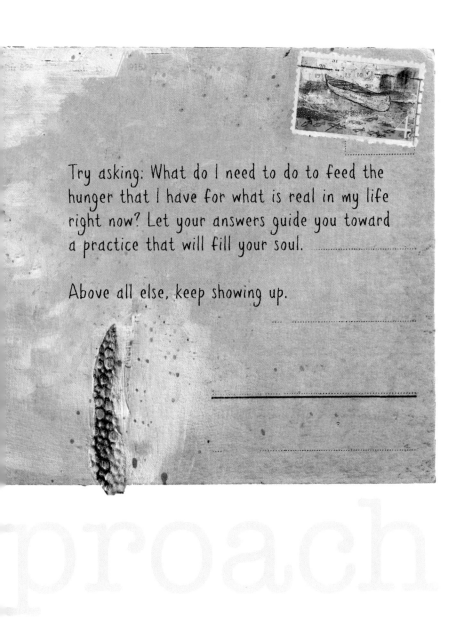

Try asking: What do I need to do to feed the hunger that I have for what is real in my life right now? Let your answers guide you toward a practice that will fill your soul.

Above all else, keep showing up.

proach

Waking Up: Attention

Sometimes I am astonished by the way my body moves in the night without my intent, and waking now, I can feel the way I've tangled everything—my ribs and arms and cheeks, everything marked with the pattern of rumpled sheets. I am lying on my side, hands pressed under the curve of my belly, wrist bones tingling with the heaviness of sleep. I hear the heat come on. Pipes rattle in the wall as hot water travels to the baseboard heater's thin metal fins that were made in a factory somewhere by huge, precise machines, operated by people wearing gloves and protective eyewear, and the warmth spreads out into the room as it does every morning, making the already-dry air drier.

The floor creaks, and I can feel the way my thudding heart makes the sheets flutter slightly, with certainty, signaling that I have arrived here again in this body, in this day. Still, I am slow to leave off dreaming, and in the time it takes me to learn again about this room (that I am in it, and must get up), I will have dreamed another dream that later I will tell my husband over coffee. It will sound disjointed and bizarre in the inevitable way that dreams sound when told out loud. It will be about him, but somewhere else, and in it I will want him in a way that I am unaccustomed to now, with my belly as round as a ball between us, and a three-year-old who still wakes us up every night. There will be an instant when his hand brushes mine as he reaches for the butter, and his skin will snag my memory. I will reach for him then, wanting everything, but already the day will have begun.

Before this, I will watch the sky spread with the sun's rosy stain, and in another minute I will pull myself upright among the covers. I will pull a robe around my shoulders and leave the place that is filled with the warmth of my husband's skin, and I will go to my desk, turn on the light, flip to a blank page, and begin to write. My mind will have no allegiance to me yet. It will still be swimming with the pictures of my dream, and words will not contain them. I will persist, following one scattered fragment of thought after the next across the page, writing in careless script, writing everything.

Here is the secret: The words don't matter yet. What matters is that I am here, writing. What matters is writing until the burrs of resistance release their hold; until my mind becomes supple, following the words, following the movement of my hand across the page. This is what I am doing: training my mind to heel like a dog until it stays close, paying attention.

The floor will be cold, and frost will have gathered at the edges of the windowsills in the night. Soon, chickadees will start to flit like sparks between the poplar and the roof, and distractions will begin to gnaw like moths at the edge of my attention. These will be the threads that will hold: my commitment to show up at the page; the thought of coffee, milky and sweet; and the way the sun tugs now at the rumpled sheet of sky, smoothing it with pale gold, and then spreading the blue of day like a promise.

And this is who I will be today: the one who gathers these threads and holds them with intention, arriving here again in this morning of my life.

Be ready for this: There will be days when nothing happens—days when you forget, or simply don't care. For me there are mornings when dawn arrives abruptly with the knobby knees of my son and my thoughts scatter before I can begin. There are other days when my mind resists waking altogether, and I burrow down deeper under the covers, sliding backwards into dreams. And of course, there are also many days when, though I am upright with coffee in my hands, I'm gone already, distracted with lists or in a rush.

It doesn't matter.

What matters is simply this: your intent to claim the day with gusto and bravery and longing. What matters is waking up and asking, *What can I be today?*, and then devoting a small handful of moments to this task of wonderment. That is all.

Go slowly as you begin the day, with the fragments of things just as they are. Your un-vacuumed floor, your rumpled sheets, your water glass smudged where your lips touched the rim. Go slowly and take notice. Feel the palm of the morning pressed against your cheek and revel in the first new rose of dawn. Wake up and allow your heart to swell with wonder.

Field Notes:
ATTENTION

attention | ə | 'ten(t) | shən (n.): the act or state of applying the mind to something; a condition for readiness for such attention involving especially a selective narrowing or focusing of consciousness and receptivity.

Consider: Everyone arrives here again and again, day after day, just as everyone dissolves with the certain and fragmented magic of sleep. While you slept, the Earth turned on its axis once again to make a brand-new day. Why are you here today?

Wake up.

In Between: Becoming

I am lying beside my son under the gabled eaves in his bedroom, and he is telling me about an alligator named Honey, who lives in the bathtub drain, and about Actulark the shark, who can shrink down small enough to swim in a teacup. He is looking up at the ceiling, and his hands are moving like a fish's fins as he describes this miniature world where anyone can be whatever shape they wish. Then he pauses, adjusts his pajamas, and turns so that his face is close to mine. His breath is sweet and warm against my cheek.

"Mama?" his voice pitches up with the question. "Where is a hammerhead shark's mouth?" And then without hesitation, as though this thought is directly connected to the next, he asks, "Also, how will the baby get out of there?" He pats my belly tenderly, his small hand tracing the hard curve that begins just below my ribs.

"I'm not sure, honey," I whisper. "But he will."

My answer is more truth than avoidance. This baby's arrival still seems improbable to me, even as my life circumvolves his a little more each day. I have become thin-skinned. Stretch marks swim like silverfish across my navel. I cry at everything.

Hormones are wreaking havoc with my moods. It is the truth that I cannot fathom what will come next, even as this baby's feet take the place of where my breath used to expand, his life already imminent in mine.

I can barely resist the urge to lunge up and dash out of this room, away from this becoming. I am impatient with the slowness of it, with the way I am here still, growing bigger and less certain. I am thirty-seven weeks pregnant and there seem to be exactly an infinite number of ways to be sucked down the drain—to fall apart; to become something new—and all of them are rushing toward me now.

These are the facts: My husband's job as a day trader has, in this crazy economic downturn, become tenuous on the best of days, devastating on the rest. My entire pregnancy can be summed up by the misnomer "morning sickness" (it lasts all day). And I am terrified of losing myself in the process of becoming a mother to two. But greater than any of these things is the way I have outgrown the definitions I've been using for my life.

Like a kid pulling on jeans for the first time after a summer of scraped knees and Popsicles and swimming, the ankles of my longing jut out bare and obvious now from beneath the minutia and obligations of my job. With each passing day spent in the low brick building of the local elementary school, this feeling has increased, and tonight I can no longer quell the feeling that I am missing my mark. This isn't my calling.

I've told everyone including myself that I'm just taking maternity leave, but tonight I know for certain: I won't be going back.

"Sing, Mama!" Liam pats my arm.

I sing again and again until the lullaby is singing itself, and my thoughts sever from the words and settle instead upon the questions of what this step will mean for my life. I sing until my mind starts circling the possibility that I might be making a terrible mistake; that this could be the stupidest thing that I have ever done. Yet somehow I know it is also possibly the bravest.

Seven years as a teacher, and suddenly in this moment I am only a version of myself that is yet to manifest. A husk, a song, a promise. A mother lying beside her son in the dark. Somebody's mother. Soon, somebody else's.

Without meaning to I stop singing, and Liam's eyes fly open.

"More songs, Mama!"

And so I begin again, doing this, being this, singing this song until I feel his body finally grow heavy, his hair damp with the sudden warmth of sleep. And beside him here, on the wings of this song, I am certain. My mind is made up. I am already in motion, already in between.

• • •

I wake to the sound of little feet, to snow falling, and to Liam launching himself into our bed, his cheeks warm, his body all elbows and knees. My body feels fragile and behemoth beside his. I've been singing "London Bridge Is Falling Down" in my dream.

"It's early," I murmur, squinting.

My husband has already gotten up, and the soft hollow where he slept beside me is no longer warm.

"I'm just going to look at you," Liam says, climbing onto the pillows, pulling his knees up to his chest. I can feel his gaze even with my eyes closed, the way he is devouring me, his mama, as though I am something he can eat.

"Hi, little one" I whisper, reaching out to rub his cheek. His hair is still damp with sweat from being curled in the cocoon of his covers.

I feel like dominos tipping toward myself, clattering back now into the slumbering weight of my body. Light spreads across the eastern sky. The baby moves against my ribs. It feels abrupt to be here again, in bed with my sleep-heavy arms, sand at the corners of my eyes.

"What are you thinking?" My voice is husky with sleep.

"I'm thinking that the moon can come to your door," he shows me with his hands. "It can come to your door and come inside. I saw it. The moon followed me in last night."

I look at him. He sits with his legs in front of him, toes pointing toward each other, and beside him on the nightstand, he's carefully set a white porcelain cup of steamed milk. Above his upper lip is a mustache of foam. He clambers off the bed, runs to his room, and comes back carrying books. And then, "I lost my bread!" he mutters, going back to retrieve his toast from whatever nook he stashed it in, and returning with it clutched in his fist along with another book.

"I'm gonna read this one first," he announces.

I still haven't figured out why he's up here with me, instead of downstairs where the morning has begun, with Todd, frying eggs in butter. But it doesn't matter. I prop myself up on an elbow and watch him.

Now he sits with his bent knees flipped out side to side, the soles of his feet pressed together, the book propped on the covers in front of him.

"The end," he singsongs in a minute, dropping the book among the covers. Then he says, "Let's snuggle, Mama," and he crawls over to me, pressing his face into the crook of my neck. With his nose smooshed under my chin, he arranges his limbs around my belly so that we're like nesting dolls, my body curving around his, and him around his brother who is still a figment of our imaginations, still unlikely magic in the stories that we tell. I can feel Liam's quick little pulse, and I can feel my own.

"Every day people ride a rocket up to the sun to check it out," Liam whispers in my ear. "And they have a hose that goes way, way, way down inside the earth that pumps up liquid that turns into fire to start the sun if it needs starting."

He tells me this so earnestly, really using the word *liquid*.

I rub my nose against his until he laughs. "That's pretty cool," I say.

Soon he leaps up again. "Look at the day, Mama!" he announces, pressing his face between the slats of the window shades with expectation. "Get up, Mama! Get up!" He chants with glee.

I am reluctant. Today more than usual. I am accustomed to being an arrow, to aiming for things: a to-do list, a target circled on a calendar page, a goal. Now there is only the baby's fluttering kicks, marking the weeks remaining until his birth like beads on an abacus. Now there are only these moments, *in medias res*. Now there is nothing for me to do except put my feet to the floor and move slowly to the window.

I too press my face between the slats and look out. I can see the moon setting, white and round like a dinner plate on the pale blue wall of the sky above the trees, and below us, on the bare tangle of lilac branches, a cardinal and a dozen jays have gathered for the seed we put out. I stand looking until the morning sunlight coming through the shades paints vermilion stripes on the insides of my eyelids. Then I shower slowly. I sway back and forth, frying eggs with thyme, and then eat them on toast with rosehip jam. I pull on boots and an oversize down jacket, and follow slowly after my husband and son as they go out to the chicken coop after breakfast, carrying leftover oatmeal and cold toast for the hens.

Inside we break the ice on the water canister, hang a heat lamp, and staple insulation over the gaps between the eaves where the wind makes the last ravelings of summer's spiderwebs flutter like torn veils in the cold air. The chickens make little crooning noises as they peck at the cracked corn that Liam pours by the scoopful into wide-mouthed bowls on the straw-strewn floor, and in the nesting boxes we find all that they have promised to the world—smooth oval eggs, some tawny and brown, others the same color as the pale winter sky.

A perfect dozen eggs on the clean metal refrigerator rack at the grocery store tells you nothing of this. Carefully packaged in Styrofoam or cardboard, labeled, scanned, it's easy to forget the harsh fragrance of soiled straw, the quiet rustle of feathers as the hens nestle in, the waiting, the effort, and then the moments just after each egg is laid, when the hen starts making a triumphant ruckus, and the whole flock joins in a cackling call-and-response. Now I slip the eggs into my pockets where my fingers trace their secrets as we walk back across the snowy yard.

Inside the house, the air is warm and smells like wood smoke. I put the eggs on the counter to be washed, and for a short while I give myself over to the task of folding the smallest laundry in the world: newborn kimono tees and onesies. The repetition helps to quiet the chatter in my heart.

Three weeks and he'll be here. Little one, something like his brother. I try to imagine his tiny hands, his eyes for the first time, what my life will be like then, abruptly. And what occurs to me now is this: No one talks about the moments in between. The moments of treading water, of moving slowly, of waiting to become. The times in between are eclipsed in the stories we tell, by the triumph and magnitude of the way things turn out or begin. But I can feel it—how the slowness of *right now* is creating the secret yolk of who I will become.

It's a hard thing—maybe one of the hardest things in the world—to just move slowly and give in to the process of becoming. Yet what I am starting to understand is that gestation is the precursor for anything new. It isn't just about having a baby. Any idea, dream, plan, or creative undertaking is the result of this same arduous work of becoming. This is what it feels like to leave your former self behind, and grow into something utterly new, like the fragile snake skins I always find in the summer by the fire pit. Every scale and sinew is etched perfectly into the transparent papery skin the snake has left, save for the open place where it slipped free to become larger than before.

This work of becoming can happen at any time, right here, in the middle of your life, with the subtlest internal shift—with acknowledging your potential.

Field Notes:

BECOMING

becoming |bi ˈkə ming| (n.):
the process of coming to be
something or of passing into
a state.

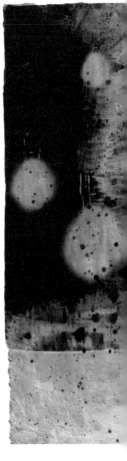

Try exploring the answers to these questions: Who are you when you slip from the scant shirt of definition? Who are you with just your open heart?

What truth comes to mind first, before labels or titles or the things you tell the world?

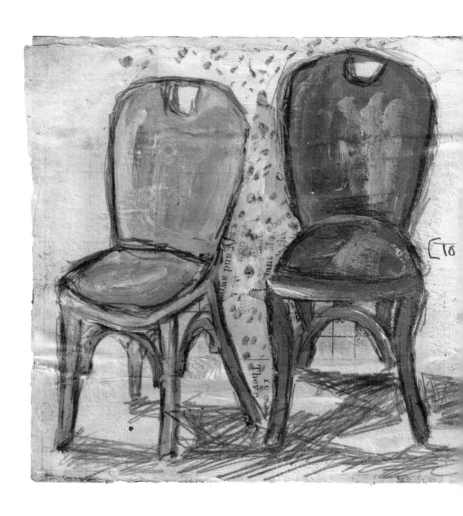

e THAN YOU aRE)

Three winters ago when we first moved here, a weasel snuck into the coop and went berserk. When I came back from buying milk and bacon and sweet oranges, I knew immediately that something had gone wrong. Todd was standing in the doorway of the coop, blood on his jeans, his face aghast, a black garbage bag in his hand. He had already gathered up the stiff bodies of the decapitated hens. It was February, long-johns weather, with a wind chill in the negative double digits.

I remember the way his eyes met mine, apologetic and protective, but also daring me to do something, so I pulled on boots and old fleece gloves and went back to the coop to help him rake out loads of blood-flecked hay, hardly saying a word.

We'd been arguing then, too. And when I saw the weasel move in the corner like the flash of dark you see mid-blink, I pushed past Todd, furious with what we'd lost.

"Go, go, go!" I yelled, yanking the hay bales back from where they were stacked along the wall. "It's behind there."

It dashed past my feet toward the opposite wall.

And though Todd did his best, grabbing a flat-headed shovel and swinging the dull blade down hard in its direction, the weasel darted quickly up the plywood wall and then behind the insulation stapled over the eaves.

We both wondered if that was the way it had come, through some small gnawed crevice, following the scent of chicken. Did it come creeping along the roost while the hens dozed, unsuspecting heads tucked beneath feathered wings? We should have noticed the signs broadcast all over. The scent of musk. The skippity tracks in the snow, not squirrel, too small for a drowsy skunk or hibernating raccoon. But we had no idea. We had no way of imagining the possibility of a thing we had yet to live through, in the same way we can't see ahead of ourselves now, as the stock market plummets and our second son is due in a matter of days.

It is the same kind of cold out now as it was then. February, with a biting wind chill, and at 4:45 it's already almost dark. Soup is steaming on the stove, and as we move about the kitchen, close like this, we pass each other expertly, avoiding any chance of touch. He carries the bread and cheese to the cutting board, I find spoons. Out of the corner of my eye I can read his tight-jawed expression. He's still running the numbers. The day on rewind: shares bought, sold, short, long.

His job is threaded on hope now, and on best-case scenarios that many days don't pan out. In the morning he puts on his luckiest T-shirt and plots his tactics and resolutions. Then he goes into his office, and by afternoon ends up losing everything he made when the day was new, while I try to go about living in the rest of the house, cooking rice and folding sheets, fear forming like plaque on my teeth.

It isn't just that this kind of domesticity makes me feel shaky in the bushel basket of my life. It's the prospect of losing even this that causes me to say *I don't know* when a friend asks me how I'm doing. I try to explain how I never pictured this—how all we talk about now are the logistics of surviving. The price of gas, what to make for dinner, or how to try again tomorrow. The fabric of our dreams that once lifted between us like a parachute feels thin. It's this that scares me. How I'm in this with everything now and can't keep us from falling.

Our words scrape like spoons at the empty bowl of these moments. We hurry through dinner, trying to keep things civil and easy for the sake of our son. Then he heads back into his office, and when we make too much of a racket in the kitchen, he closes his door.

I get it. I know why he feels like he's obligated to go back, to keep trying, to see if he can land on his feet. It's the only thing he can imagine doing. It was his first job out of college, and now the economy is slowly falling to pieces. Still. I want him to come back to us tonight. I want him to forget about work for just a little while, and dream with me of starting something new. And without really meaning to, I linger. I wipe the counters twice. I fill the dishwasher and circle the house, putting small things in their places. Finally there is nothing left to do but take Liam's hand and reluctantly climb the stairs.

"Brush your teeth," I remind him, standing at the bathroom door. My shadow is a long-legged monster across the hallway floor.

"Am I always gonna be four years older than the baby, Mama?" he asks, hopping on one foot, toothbrush in hand.

"Yup," I say, trying to hold him still to put toothpaste on his brush without his head bashing into my belly.

"My birthday will always be first then, right?" he wants to know next.

"Yours was three days ago. The baby isn't here yet, so your birthday will always come first every year," I explain, my voice harsher than I mean for it to be. But then he keeps hopping up and down as I try to help him with his pajamas, his questions lining up like airplanes in a landing pattern even after he is in bed.

Then below us in his office, Todd thunks his fist down hard. "I should have seen it," he says. "Damn it! I should have known."

He isn't really yelling, but his voice carries, and his frustration is palpable even from here. I lie beside Liam, and the words of the lullaby I am singing feel heavy like pebbles in my mouth. I try to sing. To be still. To let this moment be enough.

But Liam keeps fidgeting, and finally, after I've warned him to settle down once, twice, three times, I cannot make myself stay.

"Just ten songs, Mama!" he wails.

I've already sung more than ten, but there's no point arguing this fact. I leave him sobbing and thunder down the stairs.

Todd comes out of his office and looks up at me on the landing, expectant and confused. I push past, frustration radiating from my skin like a rash.

"Are you mad at me?" he asks, his eyes tender.

Outside the world is black now, and the windows in every room catch my reflection. I can't bring myself to look. I rush about, grabbing things: laptop, keys, notebook, shoes. It feels stupid and small to answer either yes or no. Both are true, though neither is enough. Regret already tastes like dirty snow in my mouth. My jaw aches from clenching it so tight. I want to smash my knuckles into the wall and feel it give.

"Why are you leaving?" Todd asks, running a finger along the countertop.

"I'm just leaving," I hiss. "I don't have to explain everything to you." I fumble with my jacket at the door. The thick down crumples in my arms.

"All I ever try to do is make you happy," he says now.

"I wish you wouldn't," I bark through bitten teeth. "I wish you'd try to make yourself happy instead. Name one dream you have right now. Name one." My words are grackles with sharp beaks.

"And you're so perfect," he says flatly then, the muscles tensing in his chest.

I can't say why I turned off the light and left our little boy crying. I can't explain how Todd's down days make me feel loose and uneasy inside like melting ice, or the inertia I feel now, having stopped work, though I hated it, to depend on him. I can't stop myself from feeling reckless with longing for something to happen now between us that I can't explain. And so instead I turn and go, driving over frozen ruts, under a sky full of stars, past fields spread with snow.

• • •

The weasel came back down the wall that day and made a run for the door. If I'd have been faster, I might have crushed it. As it was, I only grazed it with my boot as it fled. Then we followed its tracks out the door and around to the back of the shed where we found a fine mound of dirt heaped out onto the frozen snow.

That's always the way things are. We're always closer to the source than we expect.

We'd cased the place, hammering wood over any possible entry hole or crack, and we went to sleep that night certain the remaining hens were safe. But in the morning we heard a clucking at the back door. I grabbed a handful of oats and scooped the stray hen up effortlessly; her feathers were sleek and soft, her head eagerly bobbing toward my hand, pecking the grain. Then we saw it. Another hen on the driveway, her body still in the early-morning light.

It turned out that in our effort to prevent any further surreptitious attacks, we had somehow overlooked the obvious and left the latch on the door unfastened. The wind, blowing hard through the night, must have pushed it just enough ajar. I imagined the way the frantic hens must have fled when the weasel returned, one with its head already dangling, the others dumbly running, because that is what hens do.

I remember thinking even then that I could leave it all. Him, the hens, whatever life we were making. It was still easy to picture starting over somewhere else.

But now, I can feel the way the boundaries of my life have become blurred at the edges. Some necessary part of me has become inseparable from who we are together. This is the truth of our love now: Some days we're just in it, throwing ourselves in parallel lines above the floor. Gravity holds and then releases; some days we fall, some days we fly. But always we make a gesture between us that is greater than anything either of us could make with our own separate hands. Like a secret third body, it is something superhuman and capable of propelling us farther than either of us could reach on our own. And as I park in front of the cafe, I can feel how even now this thing between us is like a force field, a thing to be reckoned with, remarkable and necessary. As I walk into the cafe I can feel the way I have become like a boomerang, my leaving already defining the trajectory of my return.

For the sake of it, I will pay for something to eat, find a table by the gas fire, sit with my belly huge in my lap and try to write. But

I will keep glancing at the door, wanting without reason for him to walk in next, his face beaming the way it always does when he hasn't seen me for a while. Eventually I will stop trying to write and just take in the room. I will watch a lady accidentally toss her ceramic plate into the trash. She will take a step back in shock at her own mistaken brashness, unable to decide what to do. She will hesitate there, looking left and right. Then she will walk away, the cost of embarrassment more to her than the value of the plate.

After I've eaten my oatmeal raisin cookie, I will crumple the wax-paper bag it came in and stand up, my face flushing with sudden heat, and a wave of Braxton Hicks contractions will tighten around my rib cage, reminding me of all the ways this life is bigger than my own. I will stick my long arm into the trash can and retrieve the plate. Then I will wipe my fingers on a napkin, walk out into the night, and drive back toward the warmth and uncertainty that loving always means.

The coop will be quiet when I drive past, the light from a single bulb glowing from inside to make up for daylight lost. And by the front door he'll have left the porch light on.

I will find him in bed, his body turned toward the space I usually fill. I will undress quietly and slip under the covers beside him, and he will turn toward my heat and reach out his hand, and I will find it in the dark. And between us there will only be our heat, and breath, and the curve of this baby, soon to arrive.

So here it is. Our love is a mess. Our lives are awash with the driftwood of conflict. We rub at each other, and the friction sparks all my worst fears: that I am insignificant and dependent, and that the outcome of my life is beyond my control. Some days I give in to this. I let angst chase me out the door in a clatter, but the velocity of leaving slams me face-to-face into myself. I find that wherever I go, there I still am, with every fear and possible failure and shortcoming I've ever had.

This is the mistake we often make. We think, however briefly, that there might be someone else to blame for the ways that we feel small, or for the ways our lives haven't turned out the way we hoped. But the truth is, frustration and regret almost always start with some unattended ember in our own smoldering heart, and self-reliance isn't synonymous with going it alone.

Love happens in the mess, close like this, in the dark. It's not about liking, or being liked. It's not about just being okay, or faking things, or hoping things will turn out well in the end. It's about the friction and intensity of what is real, right now, and about returning time and again to the work of loving that opens your heart.

Field Notes:
BRAVERY

bravery | 'brāv rē| (n.):
the ability to take risks; confident and courageous behavior.

This is the challenge: to be brave. To find the spark of truth between you in the moment, allowing it to temper like metal forged in a smithy's hearth. Leave if you need to. Leave until you can find your breath, your pulse, your reason. Then return.

For this is what any relationship offers: the possibility to be more than you are, if you're willing to reach toward the heat and become something new.

Departure and Arrival: Conception

I am in labor. I know it the minute I wake, but I count the seconds slowly in my head to be sure. It is still dark out, and snow is falling against the windows as each contraction rolls up my rib cage like a tightening vise and then eases, marking the end of one time, the beginning of another. But this story doesn't begin here.

It began the instant that nausea washed over me as I was trying to pick the right shoes to wear for the evening, last summer in Toledo, Spain. I had a pair of espadrilles in my hand, and a pretty black-and-white dress laid out on the bed, and suddenly, all I wanted to do was curl up in a ball. It was the first time my husband and I had been away together since becoming parents, and the plan was to celebrate a friend's wedding, and then to linger poolside for a week, soaking up as much sun and sangria as possible. But there I was, blanching, and inexplicably moody. Every decision felt like an obstacle, and finally, when it was time to go out that evening, I told Todd to go ahead without me. Then when he did, I threw myself onto the bed in the dark and sobbed.

My first rational thought was that it was food poisoning. Spaniards seem to have a passion for serving things whole: red snapper, suckling pig, quail, squid. At lunch our waiter had placed an entire game hen in front of me, surrounded by broiled tomatoes and leeks. I wasn't prepared for the carcass on my plate, and though I tried to muster the necessary gusto to butcher it up and enjoy it, I could only bring myself to pick at it a little before passing it off to

Todd, who is always eager to tackle meat, whatever state it may be in. He hadn't mentioned so much as a twinge of indigestion.

My next thought, on our homeward-bound layover in Switzerland, was that I had contracted a parasite. Something in the water maybe, that was now multiplying in my gut, making my stomach clench and churn. I became absolutely convinced of this as I pushed away the perfect café au lait and chocolate croissant Todd had spent twelve euros on to cheer me up.

The feeling persisted: through landing, laundry, and little-boy kisses; through bowls of oatmeal, walks in the balmy evening air, watermelons from the vine, seltzer, naps, and jet-lag recovery.

Finally, I went to see my doctor. She listened to my symptoms with mild interest and quickly dismissed my parasite fear.

"Is there any way I could be pregnant?" I said with a laugh.

"If you're pregnant, we'd all be pregnant," she said, chuckling back. "Everyone in the office has the same IUD as you."

Then she offered another acronym: IBS. Those three letters stand for a particularly unpleasant chronic condition in which your intestinal tract behaves like a miserable coworker: uptight one minute, spewing messy details the next. And it was true, the symptoms more or less fit. Still, I wasn't convinced, and a day later, sore breasts revealed my real predicament. It didn't matter that there was only a shred of a chance. A blip. A fleeting 0.6 percent possibility of conception. You never think you will be the one when you read about those tenths of a percent on package inserts, but it has to be someone. This time it was me.

The truth is, we'd been talking with some ambivalence about having a second child for a while. But every time one of us brought it up, the timing just seemed wrong. We considered that we might be the kind of people for whom the timing is never right for having a second. We pictured our lives with a singleton, and that picture seemed more or less complete despite the nagging question of a sibling. (If you have them, you know what they're worth.) And now, suddenly, there was this irrefutable, persistent little chance, the timing of it not left up to us at all.

Maybe it's that we lack forethought. Maybe it's because we're both second kids and are used to rolling with the punches. Or maybe we're just terribly indecisive, bigger risk takers, or bigger fools. Whatever it is, we say yes together more often than we say no, and both of us have the tendency to go for things, figuring them out as we go.

And though there certainly could have been other outcomes, the one we chose was to say yes to having a second; to becoming a family of four.

Maybe every story really begins like this—in the middle, with a flicker of commitment. Maybe every story is really a spiraling timeline of arrivals and departures. Maybe time doesn't move like a spear at all, but folds instead like a ribbon, your life beginning wherever you are, again, and again, right now. Think of it. Right now is always the tipping point, always the source, the time from which all other time blooms or becomes extinct. Yet we're only in it for a brief instant, and then snap, the moment is gone. It takes longer for the mind to adjust. Our perceptions of ourselves always lag a little behind, and we arrive in the future picturing only who we were before.

We are always giving birth to future versions of ourselves.

I can feel how my life is ending and beginning in this moment here at the kitchen counter, swaying. It is 5:30 a.m. We've called his parents, and Todd has fried eggs and eaten. Between contractions I am watching the sky turn to cantaloupe, and the light of early morning spills like milk across the mountains. Inside each contraction my world is only breath and time parting for the slow arrival of something out of time. Stardust trailing, excruciating, brand-new.

When my in-laws arrive we slip out into the frosty air. I crouch down with a sharp contraction on the snowy walk, and then fold awkwardly into the car. The tops of my thighs press into the underside of my enormous belly. The heater blows against my cheeks.

"Can you believe it?" I ask, because I still can't.

He shakes his head.

The road is empty save for the taillights of a single car up ahead.

"Do you think he'll have eyelashes like Liam?"

"Maybe."

This is still true: Neither of us can picture loving this baby the way we love his brother. Our minds are less capable of imagining the future than our accordion hearts. All we know is the three of us, the winter sky, the moments we have lived. The next hours, days, years, are all blur, all fiction. And as I fiddle with the radio dial, I feel everything at once: excited, daunted, exhausted, energized. The sky grows light and clear, and the mountains bright with the snow that fell in the night.

• • •

With each contraction I become increasingly certain that the baby will arrive while I'm still in the car: that he will crown while we are waiting for a traffic light; for a bus loading early-morning passengers; for a car merging slowly just before we turn into the hospital parking lot. And then I am sure that he'll arrive right here, in the garage, as we're walking toward the large brass revolving doors. He doesn't, of course. This is just my mind playing tug-of-war with any last shred of control I think I have. Because the truth is, once you're in the process of giving birth, it's not really about you at all anymore. Birth is a manifestation of something already in motion, a collaboration with a force far greater and more inevitable than your slender, faltering will. This, at the very least, is what I've gleaned from doing it a second time.

Finally, we are in Labor and Delivery, and the morning-shift nurses hurry me to a room where I take off whatever I am wearing—each action interrupted by contractions arriving in quicker succession—and find the shower. It's here I labor like a water buffalo, lowing.

These are the things that persist: the view of rooftops, the spray of water, my husband's warm hands, and the clock across the room with its large round face. Sometimes an entire hour slips by between the minutes when I look up. Other times, forever passes, but when I look the clock has only marked a dozen minutes, moving slowly. Eventually I lose track entirely of where time begins or ends at all. I stop being myself, and am simply being.

There is no time more present than this.

And then he is.

Supple, wondrous, and alive. His little body folds against my chest, his eyes wide open, his lashes so inconceivably long that even the doctor makes a remark. His nose is smooshed and his hands seem disproportionately large, like a puppy's paws. Staring at him, I feel like he is bigger than the entire room, as though there is no way his little body can contain all that he is. This is the secret that birth offers up. We all arrive this way—greater than the smallness of the bodies that contain us, or the timelines that signify our lives.

And as my baby nuzzles into my breast, sleep smiles already fluttering across his face, my love is instant and complete, and I am overcome with joy.

This isn't just about crazy odds. We do this all the time: imagine that things are inconceivable instead of simply conceiving them and letting them grow within the bellies of our longing until they are ready to be pushed forth into the world.

Stop thinking in terms of what you think is possible. The odds are just numbers. The best things happen if you let them. Begin with saying yes. All creative work is conceived this way—with saying yes, and then persevering until the amazing and terrifying moment when you must trust the universe to reach out and accept with open palms whatever you've brought forth. Giving birth is yes in action.

Field Notes:
CONCEPTION

conception |kənˈsep shən| (n):
the forming or devising of a plan or idea;
the way in which something is perceived or
regarded; a plan or intention; understanding;
ability to imagine.

Imagine: If you could have things turn out in a way that is just exactly right for your life, what would you conceive? What would you say yes to? What would you make happen?

Start now. Every moment is an opportunity for conception.

this

Nothing Lasts: Depth

My four-year-old is perched on a stool at the kitchen counter eating eggs. He is wearing dinosaur pajamas, and when I lean over to kiss his head, I linger, pressing my face into his hair, breathing him in, he squirms away from me dramatically. He slides to the floor, colliding with an elaborate array of blocks he's constructed across the kitchen. I wince. Everything about him now is suddenly huge: his hands sticky with jam, dirt under his nails, the noise he makes, the way his arms and legs are lanky like a colt's. His need for my attention is also huge. He wants me to chase after him now. To be a pirate, an alligator, a Cyclops with my one eye only for him.

"Watch me, Mama! Watch!" he chants, swimming through his blocks, his belly on the floor.

I do not watch. Instead, I turn toward his tiny brother Rian who has begun to fuss in his little Moses basket. I gather him awkwardly, tenderly, to my chest, and am overcome by the way even this small act feels like a betrayal. These newborn days as a mother of two feel like blindness. I keep running my fingers over the surface of who I was before this, trying to locate myself here, but everything is blurry and soft like Braille on paper left out in the rain.

Sleep deprivation has me mucking about. I can't make sense of the morning's news or recollect yesterday's events. Tiredness pulls at the backs of my eyes. There is no grace in the way I make coffee now, herky-jerky, or in the way I drink it, standing at the counter, gulping, the baby cradled against my milk-stained shirt. The coffee is dark and sweet with maple syrup, but the day is already long at 9:00 a.m., and there isn't enough coffee in the world to bring things into focus.

I put the milk in the pantry. I laugh at my own lunacy.

I try again.

With a trembling hand I reach out for my firstborn's head, tousle his hair, whisper *I love you,* but he doesn't look up. I am the only one who feels unsteady now. The only one who is torn with indecision: to stay, or walk away. Necessity intervenes. The baby cries. I leave the big one among his blocks.

My ribs float in the space left vacant by this tiny boy I am holding in my arms. My weight is already abruptly less than what it was. Still, I feel like I am sinking. I carry Rian upstairs and crumple into the bed to nurse, pulling the covers up around our spooning bodies. The sheets are soft. His skin is softer. Within seconds I am slipping into a state that is neither asleep nor awake, neither swimming nor drowning. I am at the surface of rest and just beneath it, unable to let go entirely. It's the noise that keeps me here. Like something has been rewired with giving birth a second time, so that every sound filters into my brain like alarm bells. I startle at everything. I am hyper-attuned to this baby's breathing, to his slightest whimper, his smallest sigh. Beside me now he grunts and hiccups. His small hands jab at my breasts, and his nails are inexplicably sharp.

Below us on the hardwood floor, Liam's block towers crash.

I want to cry. I desperately want to sleep. And still I want these moments because I know that nothing lasts. My memory is made of pockets. Secretive, selective, and full of holes. I won't remember how it feels to have hormones take my body by storm in the middle of the night, legs drenched with sweat as I thrash at the sheets and shove my ankles out over the edge of the mattress. Or how my fingers blunder with onesie snaps in the dark, milk soaking through my shirt. I won't recall how sitting cross-legged on the bed to change a diaper, my stomach feels like it is made out of sea anemones, winnowing in the gap between my pelvis and my ribs. I will forget how it feels to have the sky grow dark now at four o'clock in the afternoon, like thick paper being wrapped around the small box of our house on this snowy hill, or how everything requires the extra effort of warmth, and it seems inevitable that every sinew and capillary in my body will be indelibly marked with the motions of preparing the fire, lighting it, banking it down each night. But soon we will be ahead of ourselves, ahead of this time. And like Penelope's tapestry, my memory will unravel with the slight tug of apple blossoms fluttering to the ground.

This palpable state of tenderness won't last. The light won't last. The winter won't last. A year from now I won't be able to recall the way it feels to have time stretch out like a rubber band and then snap back, the way it does now in this fragile, newborn time. And though I will remember these words—*urgency, love, exhaustion, wonder*—they will not adequately convey the way my body thrums now with a cellular hunger for sleep; how his milky breath is sweet against my cheek; or how his small body fits against mine, like we have always known each other, like we have always belonged together this way. And so in spite of the exhaustion I lie here wanting everything, memorizing everything.

This is what it feels like to be twirling at the very center of your life, sleep-deprived, exhilarated, terrified, consumed. It is in these moments that the present sheds its skin and the future arrives with the outlines of what you will become. You move toward it, blundering, forgetting, stumbling pell-mell, exhaustion making you desperate, reactionary, raw. Day becomes night, and night, day—the hours irreconcilable.

Remember: This will not last.

Field Notes:
DEPTH

depth |depth | (n.):
the distance from the top or surface of something to its bottom; something explored in great detail; comprehensively and thoroughly.

Go with your camera to the mirror and look. There will come a time when you will want this record, these snapshots, like a you-are-here icon, marking this moment with you in it, on the map of your life. Find good light and be gentle. Take one picture, and then another, and regard each as wondrous proof.

This is what is real right now. You, in the depths of this fleeting, immutable time.

Fight or Flight: Dialogue

I am filling the dishwasher when the squirrel catches my attention. It throws itself from the nearest tree onto the window, scrabbling uselessly, claws slipping down the glass. It is trying to reach the bird feeder, and its tail whirls, almost prehensile. It gets halfway up the window, then slides down. It tries again, and then again, until after much commotion it falls to the ground where it finally stays, nibbling the fallen shells and millet seeds the birds have dropped.

The ground is muddy, and the season's trash is laid bare everywhere, glass shards sparkling, plastic bags rustling like whispered prayers. In his office, Todd's stock positions go against him, and as he starts to lose money I can hear the clatter of his fingers hitting the keys hard, expletives slamming into the wall like darts as he tries again and again to get it right. I watch the clock, feed the boys a snack, and pace.

All day I've been waiting for something I can't quite name. For the view to change. For something sweet. For delight to maybe find me here in this house where the walls sometimes feel very close and the rooms very small, in spite of the days I get to do the work I that I love—painting, and writing freelance articles, and copyediting in the hours when my in-laws watch my kids. And today, when Todd finally comes out of his office, I turn to him, grinning, like he might be the answer.

I start to chatter brightly, but he goes to the fridge for peanut butter and then stands at the counter eating it by the spoonful, saying *Mmmm* and *Right* in the places where I pause. On days like this I know that no matter what I say, he will keep circling in the private rooms of his mind, analyzing the unavoidable errors, the unexpected market shifts, the minutia of mistakes he maybe made in predicting the ways a stock might have moved but didn't, and he'll never be fully present here with me and my eager words in our small kitchen.

If disappointment had a taste, it would be the tang you get at the back of your throat when you jump in the pool, expecting the splash and plunge, but forgetting to hold your nose. It would be the char and bitterness of burnt toast. The popcorn-flavored jelly bean when you expected lemon after pulling a pale one from the bag. And I taste it now as I bite back words. I push past him to rinse the plate I've used for buttered toast. I know that being tired like this pre-empts reason, emotion distorting everything, hyperbole becoming fact. The day has been long. We're both feeling the strain of making ends meet. We react, we react, we react.

He takes the baby now because he knows he should. I need a break. I've said as much, and he wants to be helpful. But then he lets him cry while I sit in the dining room with my laptop in the dim light and try to make a container with my words. I want them to carry me off to somewhere far away, but my fingers fumble on the keys. The sentences fall apart. The gaps between them are too wide. The crying seeps in.

In the living room Liam has built a boat out of couch cushions. He hides inside it now, talking to himself, his flashlight glinting on the walls as the wind tugs at the house, and upstairs I can hear Todd talking to the baby in the dark, but the crying doesn't stop. Outside the rain doesn't stop either. It's been falling since noon. The meadows are scabbed with melting snow.

The crying becomes unavoidable. I climb the stairs and find them in the bedroom in the dark.

"Doesn't it bother you when he cries like that?" I say, my voice tense and trembling and soft.

"He's a baby; that's what babies do," Todd spits out.

And we're off, our words moving between us like an angry swarm of bees. He watches as I take the baby from his arms. Predictably, Rian stops crying the minute he is close. He burrows into my chest and is asleep in seconds. This only makes matters worse.

"I'm pissed at him for making you mad at me," Todd says.

There is a kind of stupid logic to what he's saying, and I stare at him now, unable to think of how to reply. He stares back.

Liam has followed me upstairs, and is standing in the doorway now watching us, until we both turn on him with fierce looks and he skitters off to his room to look at picture books.

"What if we eff this up?" I ask then, softly, my body rocking back and forth in the inevitable way all parents rock, holding a baby in their arms. "What if we ruin this beautiful life?" I face him, begging for a reply, a way out, a promise. "We could, you know, if we keep up like this."

He sighs with exasperation.

It's like we're standing on rocks in the middle of a river, side by side, but slipping. We try to reach out for each other, but end up snatching at the submerged hulk of our own private fears instead.

When we're this tired, neither of us knows how to be a pillar. Todd defaults to making quick fixes, and for my part, I'm always dramatic.

Once he said, "Why do you always have to make things so epic? You're always threatening to leave. I've never once thought about that. Every fight we have isn't an indication of the end, you know. Stop making things a bigger deal than they are."

I can see how I'm doing this even now, but it's hard to pull back.

"You said you needed a break," he says, eyeing me. "I was giving you one. Then you came and told me I wasn't doing a good-enough job. I feel like I was doing the best that I could. What the hell am I supposed to do now?"

Then he says, "It's fight or flight, right? I always fight, and I guess you're always threatening flight."

I almost laugh. Is this really what we're doing? Adrenaline thundering in our veins. Are we really still this primitive after ten years of sharing bread and sleep and dreams?

Before we moved here or had children, we existed solely at the center of each other's attention. We had time then for small gifts given in boxes with colored ribbon; for the entire Sunday *Times;* for late-night movies, then pancakes at a diner. But now our days are so full we just do what needs to be done, and in uncertain times, default to doing only this. To being a function, an asset, a co-parent—each of us distracted, determined, distant. And like the coyotes that dragged one of the neighbor's sheep up the hill into the woods, we're ravenous for the fat. For extra time. For lingering. And because there is never enough time with a newborn and a four-year-old, and because we're both pushing, both exhausted, both scrambling to make ends meet, we become savage. We stake out hours, his and mine, each marking the other as the one to blame when moments go awry.

"I'm sorry for not giving you an inch," I say now, looking down at my feet. And even though it's true, it takes enormous effort to admit. But then there is this reward: the faintest glimmer of a smile at the edges of his lips. And for an instant he looks at me now, like I am the only one in the room. I put the baby in his crib, and go to Todd, my hands outstretched.

"I want to be on the same side with you," I say.

It takes both of us to move ahead. The rain has stopped and we sit together on the bed, listening to the raindrops being shaken from the branches in the wind. Waving a white flag of apology does nothing by itself. Too often we say these words to end the strife before it has really started. Too often one of us says *Sorry* before either of us really knows what we're talking about—before we get to what really matters, buried beneath what matters less.

The floor is strewn with laundry. The heater clicks on, and the radiators along the wall rattle as the steam moves through the pipes.

"I want to be on your side too," he says.

And then we hear it: an owl calling from a pine along the drive. We both wait, holding our breath. And then from somewhere farther off—maybe circling above the upper meadow, or hunting for squirrels in oaks at the edge of the dusky woods—comes a reply.

This is what I am learning, gradually, from these tenuous, aching moments of stress and longing between us: that if this time is our only time, then we owe it to each other to talk, and to try again and again to say exactly what we mean.

What other reason is there for the remarkable act of language, if not to do exactly this?

Meaning unravels in every moment. Words can always be heavy or sharp or things that fly—sticks, or rocks, or a murder of crows. But words can also be bread, and balm, and blossoms.

When we speak, we choose certain words, though our minds are full of others. And sometimes reaction and hurt are as unavoidable as the frost that will come to kill the sunflowers. Each of us is looking for a scapegoat, for someone else to blame when our own feeble attempts fall short. And on such days, silence often seems easier; or saying one thing and doing another, to make some kind of spiteful point.

But easier is not the point.

Field Notes:
DIALOGUE

dialogue | ˈdī ə lôg | (v.): take part in a conversation or discussion to resolve a problem.

If this time is our only time, and it is, I know
this: We owe it to each other to be clear.

To listen, to listen, and to reply.

Ref.C. 121

In the Thick of Things:
Discovery

The coyotes will call to the crescent moon that hangs over the roof, and in the morning, songbirds will wake the world. It will be then, between five and six, when the light is changing from gray to yellow, and the tall birch outside the window comes alive with the fluttering of wings and the scurrying of squirrels, that I will curl around my baby after nursing, and fall in love with my life. The stars will fade from the sky, the Big and Little Dippers growing faint in the yellow bowl of dreams that the day becomes, and I will wonder what my baby is dreaming about now, before language. His hair will smell like honey, like rain on a summer afternoon, like something that is mine.

His brother will find us when the sky is turning blue and the cardinals have begun marking their territory with scarlet song. He will come in dragging his raggedy blanket and shimmy in beside us, and then the bed will become a boat, a spaceship, a race car. I will stagger to catch up.

This is the kind of accounting that will take place: More coffee. Not enough sleep. A list for bananas, paper towels, milk, bread. There will be

toast with peanut butter and honey, and gold-finches sitting in a spry flock at the feeder, pecking seed. There will be three loads of laundry fresh from the dryer, in a snarl of unfolded cotton on the couch, and on the floor, the riffraff that falls when we bring in logs to stack by the stove. People's boots will make wet marks by the door. The stock market will fall. Pacifiers will get lost in the couch. And in the upstairs closet a mouse will gnaw at something in the wall, and I will hear it in moments like these when the house grows quiet.

This morning I will whirl about, carrying folded clothes upstairs, wiping counters, filling the dishwasher, making bread, embodying Newton's first law of motion—until the sun makes a chiaroscuro of shadows and bright spots on the floor, and I spread a quilt for the baby. He's started pulling his head up, and he will do this now, bare except for a diaper, his back perfectly arched, still covered in newborn fuzz. I will lie down beside him and press my nose into the warm place behind his tiny ear and whisper *I love you, I love you.*

I will watch him watch the world, head unsteady, things barely coming into focus, and for a handful of moments I will consider what it must be like to see everything this way, for the very first time. I will become absorbed, watching.

Today these things will matter: the roosters crowing, the wash tumbling in the dryer, the new grass, and the way my heart brims with more dreams for this life than it seems possible to hold.

Near noon, I will stand at the doorway watching Liam play in the mud, his pants becoming slick and spattered. And when I look in the mirror, my eyes will be pale. The color of the new spring sky. They turn this color when I am tired. Later at the kitchen window, cutting carrots, I will encounter another set of eyes. A doe, with soft brown fur, eating black sunflower shells beneath the bird feeder.

We'll watch each other for a moment, just breathing, the glass between us. Then she will stamp her hooves and dart away.

Today the peepers will make the sound of euphoria. I listen for them every spring with a kind of franticness only people who live this far north can understand, and I will hear them along the roadside in the afternoon when I leave the boys with my husband and run errands alone.

A friend once told me that when she lived in a house by a pond with thousands of peepers, the sound they made was so loud it almost made her feel insane.

"It's this sonic thrilling sound," she explained. "You just want to keep listening and listening until you feel like maybe you're losing your mind."

I know exactly what she means.

At the stoplight I will look up just as the transformer across the intersection erupts with a shower of sparks. The traffic lights will blink on and off, all down the road. And then in another few seconds, everything will simply return to the way it was. Some lights green, others red. I'll look around, curious if the other drivers saw, but no one else will be pointing in openmouthed awe. What if I hadn't looked?

At the parking garage the attendants will be talking to each other. As I pull up, the man who is not in his booth will be saying to the man in mine, "In Florida when we get a frost, all the buzzards fall out of the trees and lie on the ground like they're dead, but they're just torpid. When it gets warmer, they wake up again."

He will actually use the word *torpid*. This will delight me to no end, though when I look it up later, I will find no proof. Only that when there is a frost in Florida, it's the lizards that are torpid, and the buzzards are sure to have a feast on them.

Later, at the grocery store, a little girl with Down syndrome wearing a white ruffled dress and butterfly wings will be following after her mother. Her mother's jacket will be on inside out, and the girl will insist on a heavy green watermelon, plunking it into the cart alongside other more sensible things: bread, fish sticks, shampoo, eggs. And at the cafe in the bookstore I will see a middle-aged woman offer a cupcake from a white to-go box to an old man who is sitting alone with a Band-Aid on his bulbous nose. His face will erupt with delight. He will say yes. Across the cafe another man will look just enough like my father that when he looks up at me and smiles, I will smile back, unguarded, tears fresh on my cheeks with a sudden rush of grief. In moments like these I'm always caught off guard by the fact that I'll never get to talk with my father again, though it has been almost a decade since he died.

On the way home, a dozen college boys will be running on the muddy grass in the median. And even though it's still cold out, they will be shirtless, their lithe backs gleaming with sweat, shoulders flung back, feet lifting off the ground as though at any minute they might simply fly away.

When I return with paper sacks of groceries, the mail, and cracked corn in a fifty-pound bag for the hens, these things will count: the metal wind-up robot by the door, the paint still on my fingers from finishing a canvas the night before, and the plate of oranges on the counter, gleaming in the late-afternoon sun.

Today, noticing will matter. In the thick of things each instant will be filled with ache and sweetness, like honey on a waxy comb and the bee sting, both. Today the moments will ask for wonder, for careful consideration, for sacrifice, for joy.

What might happen if you really paused in the middle of what you are doing and looked around? What unexpected wonder is waiting in the grass? What solace waits to be noticed at the stoplight, at the curb?

I know that I stop seeing, really *seeing*, when I am preoccupied and rushing about. When I feel the hours slipping away, when work calls, when errands demand completion. Yet this life asks for wonder, for steadfastness, for taking note.

How else do you think moments of beauty will find you, if not like this? With salt thrown over a shoulder, or umbrellas not opened indoors? Luck has nothing to do with finding moments of grace or ease.

How to recalibrate your attention: 1) Squeeze your eyes shut, and when you open them, look like you are seeing for the first time. Look, really look, at what is in front of you right now. 2) Feel the air on your face. Fill your lungs. Touch whatever is at hand: the ground beneath you, branches, spoons, spilled jam. 3) Use your camera as a lens for discovering the possibility for beauty right here. Capture the galaxy of crumbs on the table, the row of forks in the sink, your cat mid-yawn, tulips in a jar. 4) Consider how every single thing is distinct—every blue jay, every pebble, every leaf.

See everything as an opportunity to be amazed.

Field Notes:
DISCOVERY

discovery |dis ˈkə v(ə)rē| (v.): to find (something or someone) unexpectedly; to become aware.

Growing Pains: Fervor

When I am just finally, mostly asleep after two fit-ful hours of waking and nursing, my nose pressed against the baby's warm head, Liam arrives with an armload of trains and maneuvers them under the covers. Today I am resentful of his racket—of the way my day must always start with his.

"Go back to your room," I murmur, my voice gravelly, nudging his small body with my knee.

Then suddenly he is throwing up.

It smells putrid and sickly, and I yell for Todd who is in the bathroom. He brings towels and puts Liam in the shower, then takes the soiled sheets downstairs while I dry Liam's shaky arms and legs and put him in a fresh pair of pajamas.

And so the day becomes a detour.

When I go downstairs, I see that another unexpected thing has occurred in the yard. The goose has hatched a chicken's egg, and now there is a frail bundle of feathers and fluff to contend with. Its feet are the size of a sparrow's, and its wings flap uselessly as it tries to follow its unlikely mother about. The goose leaves the chick cheep-ing pitifully in the middle of the rain-drenched lawn and lifts into the air. She flies low over the

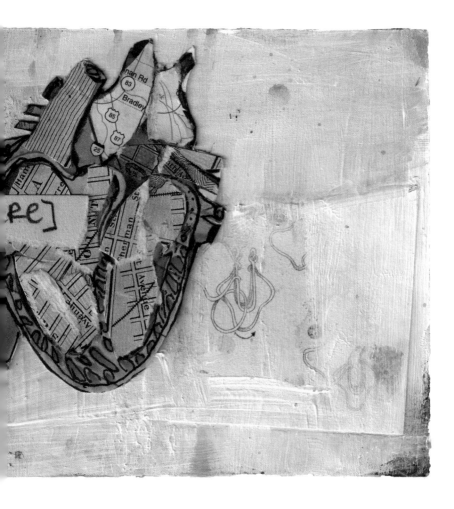

grass to the galvanized tub of water that we fill for her and plunges in like she is reuniting with a lover, clear beads of water falling from her feathers, the chick left far behind.

She got broody just as the sap started to run. Gathering straw into a nest at the corner of the coop as the world reluctantly thawed, mud everywhere, the greening lawn newly exposed to sky. Then she stole five or six eggs from the flighty hens, and soon we found her sitting all day long, the eggs nudged possessively beneath her heavy gray breast. This goose is the stalwart remainder of the three Toulouse geese we started with last spring. Foxes took the other two by their long necks at dusk in the summer, and all winter this one mourned, hankering for company, and come spring, for this.

I planned to take the eggs away from her one afternoon when she left the nest briefly, but at the last minute I let her keep one, and now it has hatched.

I can't explain what made me change my mind, except to say that in that moment I felt like I could understand her plight: how it's possible to long for something, and be repulsed by it in the next instant; how it feels to crave tenderness and domesticity, and then to want to fiercely buck it off. This is instinct, the tug of fear and longing in tandem. The way every cell in my body responds to the needs of these two boys that are mine now—milk filling my breasts; my body moving in a sudden sprint to catch the big one as he stumbles now, going down the stairs. In one instant my heart gives itself over to the pummeling of my children's incessant need for me, their hunger for my affection, their craving to be close. Then in the next, self-preservation kicks in, and I lock myself in my studio to write or paint for as many hours as I can before the baby needs to nurse.

Loving a child isn't like loving an equal. Instead, it is animal and complete. It comes from somewhere in you that is unconditional and beyond reason, plundering your heart until your entire being can do nothing but vibrate in harmony with this love song of impulse.

• • •

The day has slipped past, and by nightfall Liam has stopped throwing up, although his fever persists. Tucked into bed he dozes, then sleep-wakes.

"The yellow dog!" he shrieks, pointing out into his room where trains stand in rows on wooden tracks and chalk rests on the easel tray for another day of play. "Get that yellow dog!" He is breathing fast.

"Here, drink some water," I say softly, holding a glass to his dry lips.

When he drinks he wakes all the way up. "Hi, Mama," he whispers in recognition. "I love you."

"I love you too, baby," I say, helping him back onto his pillows.

He sleeps again and calls out again, and in the morning when he crawls into our bed, he doesn't look rested at all. His cheeks are flat. His eyes have no sparkle.

"I'm feeling much better," he says hopefully, reading the ill-concealed worry on my face.

But after eating a few bites of toast he turns away. "My tummy still hurts," he says softly, disappointed.

The chick has also survived the night, but today it is pouring. The goose doesn't stop at the rain, and the downy chick becomes so damp and weak, it can only stand in one place, calling and calling after the goose as she moves ahead with big strides, her neck snaking out among the raindrops to peck at plantain and dandelions, honking again and again for the chick to follow after. I'm sure some part of her knows that it's her baby. She makes soft throaty noises when it's near, and lets it sleep on her back after she's through with preening. But then she leaves it just the same.

I want desperately to get involved, to rescue the chick and force the wayward goose back to the nest. I also want to do away with the whole thing. The chick. The goose. The entire predicament, and the way I'm in it, too.

Until you're in it you can't comprehend the cipher of guilt and fear and longing that instinct scrawls across your days as a parent. At least, I could never imagine the way it feels now to rub Liam's back. His scapula are like sharp clay wings, and I can count each of his ribs like the hull of a canoe that is drifting away from me on feverish eddies of sleep. He's been sick so often in the past six months that I have begun to falter. I can't shake the feeling that something is off—that something is really wrong. We've taken him to the doctor and done everything that anyone has recommended in succession— antibiotics, homeopathy, chiropractic—and still, he's been sick every month since November.

Now his eyes are dark and the glands in his neck are swollen. The fluid in his ears has become a perfect haven for repeated infection, and at our last doctor's visit, his hearing was temporarily diminished by almost twenty decibels.

"What?" he asks after everything I say, watching my lips as they move. "What?"

Everything sounds like it is underwater to him, and feels like it is underwater to me.

Outside, the rain keeps falling, and water fills every depression in the stones along the front walk. The chick is shrill and persistent with its calling, the goose even louder when she calls back. All day this back-and-forth continues, the goose calling and then the chick, until in desperation I scoop the little thing up and put it in a shoe box by the woodstove. I offer it fresh water and mash, but it refuses everything and drives me crazy with its pining, until finally I lure the goose back to her nest with another egg.

Though she doesn't get how to care for this odd baby that she's hatched, she's a sucker for the egg, and goes straightaway to the nest, plopping herself heavily onto the soft circle of hay that I've made, her instincts only half intact.

I get it. I watch her with empathy and contempt. *You left your baby, you stupid thing!* I want to scream at her. But just the same, I reach to stroke her long, elegant neck. I know what it feels like to want to fly away.

I am not good at this. Simply being here next to my son on the couch, proffering a damp washcloth, a slice of apple, a sip of water. I'm used to divvying up my time judiciously, hoarding some for myself. E-mail. Exercise. Facebook. Bookstores. Errands. Bills. Laundry. Paper mail. Lattes. Bad moods. Mopping. Moping. Making love. Arguments. Paperbacks. Phone calls. Sit-ups. Writing. Waistlines. Mileage. Mice behind the baseboard. Worry. It all seems so indulgent now, as if any of these things matter at all when we're here imagining this:

Leukemia.

He has almost every symptom, and suddenly my vision is a zebra's back. This is another kind of falling in love. Desperate. Consuming. Vertigo. The Internet doesn't help, and my imagination runs wild as each new search reveals more symptoms, more sure signs. I become ever more convinced as I listen to him cough; find a small bruise on his left knee;

and try to coax him with food, though he abstains, disheartened, holding his stomach. I imagine the future, and how these moments could be the beginning of everything.

The baby sleeps unknowingly on my chest, hale and warm, and I picture his babyhood suddenly illuminated by fluorescent hospital lights, eclipsed by his brother's illness. Every parent does this at some point, this frantic, panicked picturing. Fast-forward. Worst-case scenario. I feel like a starfish now, the belly of my worry distended and translucent, consuming everything.

• • •

The morning of the third day is clear and warm, but when I go to the coop I find the chick still and silent in the corner of the nest, the goose disconsolate. She looks up at me with her yellow eyes, her neck shaking, and hisses at my invasion. Then she leaves in a clatter of frustration, her huge wings beating the air. I carry the chick to the bank at the back of the house and bury it among the ferns. The goose keeps her distance, but then she follows me to the door when I go inside and spends the morning there, calling and calling for what she's lost.

Inside I call the doctor again, and when we arrive at his office, he is patient with our worry. He must be used to facing parents like us in the exam room. Our eyes are ringed from lack of sleep.

"It's been the same thing for everyone," he assures us. "It's just been one heck of a season. One of the worst on record. Everyone has been getting sick again and again."

We nod. Maybe. But what if it isn't the case? What if it's more?

"Okay," he agrees. "We'll do a blood test to be sure."

On the way to the lab we get Liam a cherry-flavored Tootsie Pop, and when it's his turn to have blood drawn he sucks on it and we hold his hands. He doesn't cry. The lab techs are astounded. We fold around him like paper cranes. Afterwards we go to the toy store and buy the biggest monstrosity of a remote-control truck we can find. We thrive on his fleeting smiles. We wait.

Worry like this makes the rest of my life stand out in stark contrast. It's easy to make out what matters now, among the jostle of other unimportant things. Simply: to have each other; to love; to have mornings with elbows and knees and laughter, despite too little sleep. To feel the way each day my heart expands because of them, sometimes until it aches—other times till it is brimming with incalculable joy. This is everything.

• • •

Later when the sun is high and the mud wasps have hatched and are buzzing drowsily about the stone wall at the front of the house like heavy little helicopters, and the goose has grown quiet, her head tucked beneath a wing in the shade, the nurse calls with the results.

He's just sick.

"It's just been a terrible winter, really," she says, laughing at the sound of relief in my voice. I want to press my face into the warm ground.

When Liam wakes from his nap I kiss his forehead and rub my nose into his neck until he pushes me away, giggling weakly. Outside the sky is the color of bluebells, and along the road coltsfoot has come up like a thousand little suns.

It can begin with anything. It can begin with a tiny bump on your arm; as dark circles under your eyes; or something quiet and secret and soft—a tumor, maybe, in the belly of someone you love, which was the way it began with my father, ending quickly three months later with full-blown pancreatic cancer.

It can arrive at any time—the message that this entire life of yours is up for grabs, not really yours at all, but rather some brief gift you occupy with cells and soul and longing.

Don't wait for this. Act now.

Field Notes:
FERVOR

fervor | ˈfər vər | (n.):
great warmth and intensity of emotion; a passionate feeling; enthusiasm.

Ask: What is precious? Of all
the things that you hold, with
everything tugging you in a
hundred directions at once,
what really matters? Then
consider: What would it look
like to live toward what
matters with everything
you have?

Begin immediately.

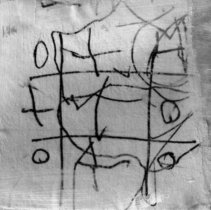

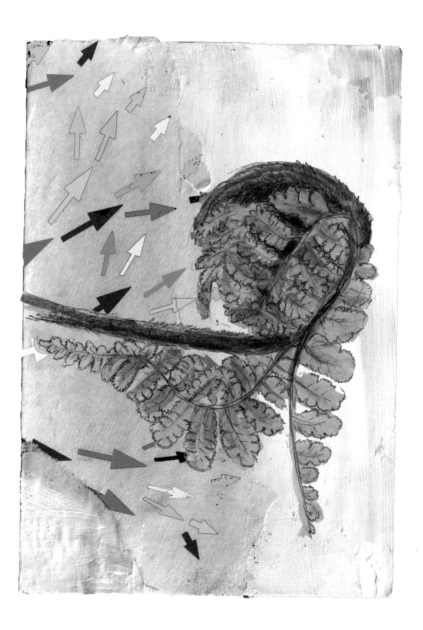

Moving to Be Still: Habit

It takes concentration to articulate my slender ankles over the rocks, the sun hot on my shoulders as I run through pockets of warm air, sweet with the fragrance of grass; past a field of placid-faced cows; past a passel of neighbor boys playing catch, the redheaded little brother's hair gleaming in the sun as if it has been lit on fire. I have been running for close to thirty minutes, and now I'm on the return stretch, passing mailboxes every fifteen yards or so. I am so close I can see our mailbox in the distance, there below a spreading oak, but the road pitches up here slightly, and the final stretch is all uphill. I want to give up.

How easily I default to this when something starts feeling hard. My Loki brain tells me it's not possible to finish. This last thousand yards is suddenly an impossible distance, and I can feel the way my mind is becoming frantic. *You can't do it. Stop now. This is too hard. Stop pushing. Stop. Stop.* My breath is ragged. All I can feel is the rawness in my lungs, the ache in my left knee, the fire in my quads. Who cares if you finish or not anyway? Just give up. And for a handful of seconds I hesitate, my feet slowing.

Then I refocus on my breath. I narrow my gaze until it is just in front of me—until the road becomes a smooth blur moving under my feet. I imagine my feet lifting effortlessly as though the ground were a treadmill, and I am simply standing on it and lifting up my feet. Left foot, right foot, left, right. Gradually I slip into a cleft between the seconds, where my mind no longer chatters and my body simply does. One, two, three, four. Heartbeat, breath, heartbeat, breath. Soon there is only the *thunk thunk thunk* of my running feet, the goldfinches lifting in yellow flight from the thistles, the gravel. And if I can stay here, in this groove of focus, and can empty my mind of everything so that I am only muscle and breath and attention, then I can finish.

Today: Four miles.

• • •

I started the habit of running when my belly was soft and my legs were shaky, just six weeks after the birth of my second son. It was barely spring and the roads were soft with mud. I would run two miles at first, then gradually three, repeating the process each day because sometimes it was my only time, the only thirty minutes that were entirely mine, uninterrupted. Other days it was just about grit and stubbornly persisting, about proving something to myself. Even when it rained for weeks, even when the worry felt endless and self-doubt puckered the edges of each ripe moment, I would go running and feel the way my rib cage would rise and fall, my lungs performing the miraculous exchange of oxygen and air. And gradually it became a kind of proof-positive for my life: If I could run even when I didn't feel like it, and keep going when I wanted to give up and my head was an inferno of doubt and despair, then I could persist with everything else. If I could run, then I could wipe sticky cheeks, tell stories, kiss scraped knees, make plum tarts, shuck peas, pitch potential freelance articles, find four-leaf clovers, find hope, drink lemonade, drink coffee, put words down, hit the delete key, remember, recycle, rinse the plates, stay up late, write, write, write, run.

Now I am running with the sun on my face. Ferns, like green paper cutouts, are everywhere along the roadside. The ground is damp and the gravel sings underfoot. I can feel the way my quads have loosened, my legs finding a pace where they are moving on their own, one foot in front of the other, lungs gratefully winnowing each inhalation of sweet air. Then I am back, passing the final mile-marker tree with its shaggy bark, tall by the mailboxes where the road is cool with shade. Momentum carries me farther: past the neighbor's sheep barn, where wild blackberries are ripening in the ditch. I pick some, the juice staining my fingers, and then loop back, walking now, my heart still thudding hard as endorphins pump through my bloodstream in triumph.

I'll be honest: Some days I wake up already wanting to put my fist through the wall, and running is the very last thing I want to do. There are days when I hate the sound of my children and the sound of the crows in the trees. And mornings when my thoughts are frail and jagged, and coffee seems like a weak substitute for all the hours I did not sleep. But it is on these days that running matters most. To simply run, expecting nothing, and gradually mark the difference. To move one foot and then the other, in a steady rhythm, feeling my lungs and heart sending bright red blood circling through alveoli and capillaries, until I feel right with my life, with the moving sap, with the windy fields, with all my hopes.

It is something to run every day without exception. To leave the house, run, and gradually mark the difference. To find strength in this act of momentum and stillness. I can't quite explain what happens—how running daily has rearranged something in my very core; how nothing compares with this feeling of strength.

I'm telling you this on purpose.

We're stationary too often while our minds run amok, fear and resistance making an awful clatter. But we are meant to move. One foot, then the other foot, the mind growing still. You can find solace here, and the bold courage that comes from persistence.

This isn't about exercise. It isn't about losing weight, or car-
diovascular health, or altering your body mass index. It isn't about
being an athlete, or even about running at all. And it certainly isn't
about being efficient, squeezing every ounce of capability out of the
moment. It is not the same to read a book on the elliptical, or to plug
in headphones so you can whitewash the moment with song. This
is about making a habit of being between movement and stillness,
right here.

Field Notes:
HABIT

habit | ˈha bət | (n.):
a settled or regular tendency or practice; a
general form or mode of growth.

Try moving every day for a week without exception. Move long enough for your body to remember that this is what it is made to do. Move outdoors where the air might be damp and sweet with bloom and fruit, or thick with traffic, or dust, or frost. Don't think of multitasking.

Just move every day without excuses, without giving up, until you are simply here.

The Moment at Hand:
Hunger

I am at the pottery studio. The light is yellow, the room whirring with wheels, clay slick on my hands. I am learning how to center and to be centered. I am throwing my weight forward from my hip through my elbow into the clay circling under my palms, until it becomes even, and steady. Until the hunk of clay under my palms is round and still at the center of the wheel. Then it is ready to be drawn upwards and outwards into the shape it will become.

This requires unwavering commitment.

Once you've taken hold of the clay and have begun to draw it up, you can't stop, or second-guess, or let go, or wonder. You just have to persist. You have to take the clay and steadily move it upwards, concentrating only there, on the lines formed by pulling the clay slowly toward the heavens, the metal of the wheel circling under the outside edge of your palm. You have to take the clay between the forefinger of your left hand and the bent knuckle of the forefinger on your right hand and bring it up in one steady fluid motion.

possib

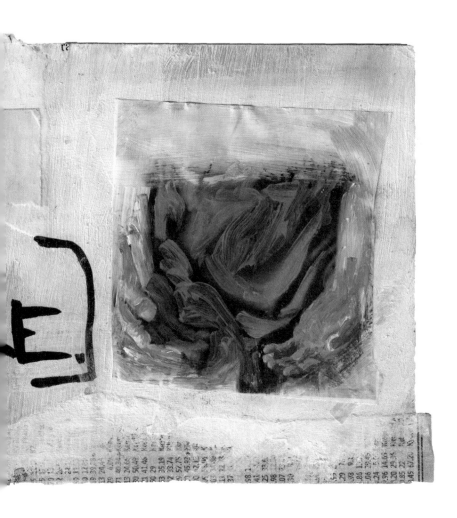

This is damn hard. Second-guessing ruins everything. Any pause, distraction, or hesitation will immediately be evident. Your throw lines will become irregular, or worse, the entire piece will suddenly jilt off center and begin to flap and flail like a dervish might, until it invariably collapses.

This is what my hands are slowly teaching me: that I must be centered first, and then open to the endless act of being drawn upwards toward who I am becoming.

Also this: The first ten things I make will be crap. Likely, the first hundred things I make will be crap. But it doesn't matter. What matters are my fingers moving and the clay beneath them. What matters is practicing this movement again and again, clay slipping through the curve of my hands.

It's easy to have big dreams: bowls fit for leafy salads, vases tall enough for lilies on the stem. Being humble is harder. Learning to respond to the clay with steady breath and an unfaltering hand is harder still. Yet I can feel how my soul begs for this careful work, for the fullness of touch, for the messiness of making. Even as I hungrily devour the world with my eyes, everything there at the ready for me on the screen with the click of a button, this is also true: It is my hands that make things real. Brushstrokes or lines on the page, bowls, bread, sensation, wonder. Each articulating bone following the logic of touch, the splendor of intention.

Often I forget that it is my hands that bring me here, to this singular moment. When the day is full of digital circumstance—fifty-three e-mails in my in-box, an iPhone fully loaded, a desktop of bookmarks, Pinterest, Vimeo, Hulu—it is so easy to let the day slip by without bringing attention to my hands and the work that they do to sustain me.

Tonight I watch a tall man with a scruffy blond beard and bright blue eyes work patiently for hours, making a dozen perfect bowls. Each one is wide, symmetrical, impossibly delicate, deep. He catches my eye, probably because I've been staring for a while at the cylinder he's thrown with even lines, the clay the same thickness from base to rim.

"It's beautiful," I say, nodding.

He doesn't pause, but a smile moves briefly across his face like a sudden flight of sparrows.

"Thanks," he says.

His hands never stop moving. And just like that he slips back into the quiet groove of concentration he was in.

I am beginning to learn that this is what mastery is about: a quiet, unwavering focus on the moment at hand, on the smooth red clay circling through my fingers at a speed faster than birds fly. If you use too much water, the clay becomes too pliant and soft. It gives too easily under your uncertain hand. It buckles or collapses. If you use too little water, your hand will burn as it rubs along the clay, friction making it quickly hot. Then chunks will rip away irregularly from the outer edge, and the piece will stagger off center.

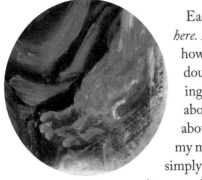

Each time I am here, I try to just *be here*. And it is painful, almost, to observe how often I hesitate, or second-guess, doubting what I am capable of making. What I am trying to do here is about getting out of my own way, about moving beyond the chatter of my mind without flinching. My intent is simply to take hold of the clay and move it up continuously, regardless of what I think.

Of the 206 bones in your body, more than 50 of them are in your hands. Doesn't this astound you? Isn't this reason enough to put aside a handful of moments for doing purposeful work with your hands? Rumi says, Let the beauty we love be what we do. Today let it be this:

Make bread.

Start early enough so that it will have time to rise on a sunny windowsill for a few hours. Mix the flour, salt, olive oil, yeast, and water in a large bowl, and then gather the dough with your hands. The point isn't the bread. The point is kneading. The point is doing this work with your hands.

Knead, and add flour as needed (a cup or so as necessary), until it becomes supple in your fingers. Give yourself over entirely to the rhythm of kneading. Pay attention to the way your fingers move with the dough. Knead until it becomes elastic, until it stretches easily. Knead until you feel your attention settle on this simple, honest work.

Rinse the bowl in warm water, drizzle it with a little olive oil, and turn the dough in it once, so that it glistens with oil. Cover it with a clean towel and place it somewhere warm; then, go about the work of your day as the dough begins to rise.

When the dough has doubled in size, press it down gently with your fingers and form it into two loaves. Put these in clay bread pans if you have them, or on a cookie sheet if you don't. Let them rise again until nearly doubled. Bake at 375 degrees for about forty-five minutes.

Eat the bread warm, with butter, and be grateful.

Bread for Right Now

3 cups warm water
1 tablespoon sea salt
1 tablespoon instant yeast
6 tablespoons olive oil
4 cups bread flour
2 cups whole wheat, oat, or other flour

(Makes three loaves—or two loaves and one large pizza.)

Field Notes:
HUNGER

hunger | ˈhəng gər | (v.):
to have a strong desire or craving
for something.

Lines and Sparks:
Hurdle

I grew up with stories; we all do. But this one in particular was mine: that I was born at the wrong time. That it is possible to regret your children— that your life could be made irrevocably smaller because of having them.

This was my mother's story about me. "You and your father have always had a connection," she said countless times when I was growing up.

Sometimes she would use this as leverage against me, particularly as a teenager. "When you came, he didn't need me in the same way. He used to sing you to sleep every night, and when you cried he would rock you in your bassinet." As if this were some kind of betrayal. As if there wasn't enough of his love for the both of us. As if I had a choice in any of it at all.

Later, by way of explanation for her depression during my teenage years, she would say, "You just came along so quickly." There was a certain matter-of-factness in the way she'd say this. "I look back and wish I'd had some time with him to work on the things we imagined were possible

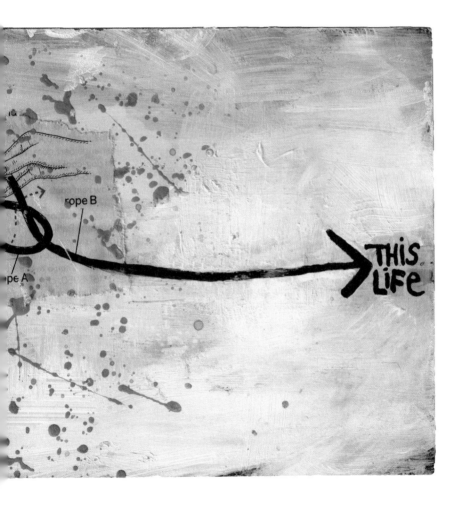

back then. If you'd have come later, everything between your father and me would have been different."

By adulthood I realized that this wasn't just her story. It happens everywhere. Maybe it's not always told so personally, but it has the same implications. It is passed down through the generations, and across them. Many women I greatly admire—writers and artists and athletes—have confirmed what I learned by heart: Children are a sacrifice, a forever debt against your independence. A natural disaster. A way to lose sight entirely of who you are. Or even a cop-out ... as if by having them, you were throwing in the towel and voluntarily making your life smaller.

As I listened to these women, I became convinced that unless everything was carefully planned out and timed, my life would essentially be over if I had children. And even though I had always pictured my life with children in it, I spent a lot of time dreading their possible arrival and imagining how it might actually be best to avoid having them altogether.

But when my sons did come along, a different story emerged. I think I'm still getting over my surprise that it isn't the same as my mother's. Her story—*You'll never really feel like yourself again*—isn't my story at all.

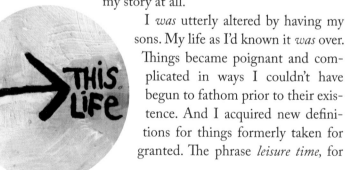

I *was* utterly altered by having my sons. My life as I'd known it *was* over. Things became poignant and complicated in ways I couldn't have begun to fathom prior to their existence. And I acquired new definitions for things formerly taken for granted. The phrase *leisure time*, for example, has been undeniably altered, and *sleeping in* now means waking up at 6:30 a.m. instead of at 5:00 a.m. A good night of sleep is measured now by the number of interruptions, rather than by the number of hours actually spent asleep. And there is a set of task-specific skills that parenting requires that I am mostly terrible at, the least of which are these: stain-treating shirts, emptying pockets before throwing pants into the wash, remembering snacks (and tissues, and wipes) every time I leave the house, and keeping itty-bitty socks in pairs.

But there is also this: Becoming a parent has forced me to listen again and again to my stirring heart in a way I never did before. It has propelled me toward my creative work with the kind of awesome advantage that female athletes have after having a baby, where the very biological state of pregnancy and the immediate weeks postpartum provide a real physical advantage. More blood, more oxygen, quicker recovery.

Before I had them, children were more or less abstractions in my mind—a part of the *Someday* that would happen after I had *Accomplished Things*. It was in that same Someday that I envisioned myself as a writer, while I filled the present tense with more seemingly pressing things: commuting, landscaping, sitcoms, dry cleaning.

Then my boys showed up. Both unplanned, born four years and four days apart, as though they were in cahoots to teach me things right from the start.

When I look back on my life before them, I laugh at the way I squandered my time. I made excuses often, and pushed my creative work to the side because I always felt like I could pick it up at some future, more-convenient time. There was always the promise of another night, another day, equally ripe with hours. Because I had so much time, I often missed the value of each hour, each day distilled into minutes slipping by.

Now my time is compressed. The very fact that I am not always at the center of my own life is what spurs me to acknowledge the only Someday I'll ever have is right now, and to dig in. Having children forces me to consider my life through the urgent lens of the present, and under that intense regard my creative work continues to surface, as persistent and indisputable as my need to breathe. My children compel me to live voraciously; and when I'm not with them, each slender moment becomes burnished and bright.

I don't want anything more than this: to be a mother and an artist both.

Each state of being informs the other. My children fuel my creative spark, far more than they ever quell it, and each day with them I am the line, and the one that draws the line—the spark, and the match that is struck.

There is a word that I love which describes what this is like: *equipoise.* I love it for its onomatopoeia and for the way it describes the way I am now: tilting back and forth between my creative work, and the work of mothering my two sons. This is not a static state of affairs, a thing you achieve once and then can simply maintain. Rather, it is an ongoing process of leaning wholeheartedly toward whatever is at hand. It also means that my house is a mess, the laundry never folded.

Still, balancing this life is like walking a slack line between two trees. The minute you put your foot onto the line it starts to quiver, and then your muscles bunch and tremble in response. To stay up there, moving one foot in front of the other above the ground, is an act of simultaneous stillness and movement—of breath held, and breath released; of resistance and ease. It requires absolute commitment to whatever is immediately there: the breeze, the line, the muscles in your calves. And you can never get too cocky or sure, for the minute you think you have it, everything starts quivering anew. The line begins to shake as if of its own accord. The more it shakes, the more your body vibrates in response.

What my children ask for and what creative work requires is the same: attention, humor, commitment. Now if the moments offer quiet, I write—no excuses. If the moments offer clatter, I get down on the floor with the boys.

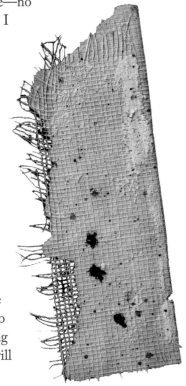

• • •

On the phone today my sister said, "Getting married is already such a sacrifice; I'm just not sure about having a kid."

Recently every conversation we've had has been about having children. She's on the fence, while her husband is leaning toward a baby.

She says, "Having a baby is just this huge decision to sacrifice your life." Like me, she's heard the stories. Like me, she is independent almost to a flaw.

These are the things she thinks are on the line: a successful career, abs to die for, and the ability to make a thing happen just by throwing all your will behind it.

"I hear you," I say, pressing my lips into my baby's soft hair as I cradle the phone to my ear. "I get that you're worried about losing what you've fought for, I really do. But that isn't the only possible outcome. Promise."

I try to explain how my children's blooming, galloping lives create a context for mine, for the things that matter, for the way this life is passing. How the birth of each son prompted me to take huge affirmative actions toward a more fulfilling life.

With my firstborn, we moved from suburbia to the end of this long dirt road here, where the fields fill me with wonder. With my second, I've started, finally, to do the creative work that makes me feel fulfilled. I am in better shape now than I have ever been in my life. I can run farther and faster than I ever have. And while I don't climb many mountains now, danger has never really been a thing I crave, but depth is, and I've found it here in this life.

I arrived at actual motherhood by accident in the same way my mother must have, with both my children confounding the odds of contraception. But the truth is, the part of me that always imagined being a mother also imagined that motherhood could be like this—and maybe that's the difference. What I know now is that my mother didn't mean to say that she regretted having me. What she regretted was not claiming—sooner, and with more intention— what her life could have been with the man she loved.

Stories are powerful things. What we make of our lives is whatever we imagine. I didn't start out believing this story was possible, but I started out believing that it *might* be, and here it is: Children are like weeds in a sidewalk. They grow tall and leggy in an instant, splitting you wide with love and possibility.

I don't know how to shuck an oyster, deep-sea dive, wear a space suit, read tax code, or order clever drinks at a bar. I don't know how to play Ping-Pong or hang-glide, and I don't know how to fish. But I am learning how to reel this slender line, balancing in thigh-high waders, surrounded by the splashing my boys make in my life. And this is what I want to tell you: If your intention is to become the most that you can be in this lifetime, then having children will not stop you.

Obstacles are mostly things we create in our minds, and if what you long for is joy and abundance, then let it be measured by how far you can bend, and how gracefully you can move around the hurdles. Life isn't meant to be lived in equal parts, with each thing accounting in equal measure for the other.

Some days it takes everything I have simply to move forward without leaving anything behind: coffee mugs on the roof of my car, appointments, tenderness. Other days, more is possible. What I am trying to say is this: It's easy to look at what is achievable in a single day and always come up short. But it is just as easy to underestimate what you can accomplish in a year.

Field Notes:
HURDLE

hurdle | ˈhər dəl | (n.):
a barrier, or difficult problem to
be overcome; obstacle.

Whatever the work is that you long to do, do it today without excuses. Involve your children if that is the only way. My studio is always a riot of snippets, their paintings always strewn about my floor. Begin with pouring yourself wholly into whatever you are doing, and trust that momentum will gather, that resources will arrive.

Opportunity will find you.

passionate

Give-and-Take: Intersection

In bed, the sheets unwashed, the windows open wide to the thrumming sounds of night: crickets, beetles the size of a child's fist buzzing drunkenly about, fat winged moths, bats darting in zigzags in the grassy air. We lie breathing, side by side. Then I turn to face you, my lips brushing your collarbone, your shoulder. Salt from the day's run is slick on your skin.

These are days of dwindling sun and sweet tall grass; goldenrod allergies, runny noses, snot wiped onto the back of a calloused hand while we're out splitting wood, dirt under fingernails. We run in the afternoons, two miles, three, four. We lie on the madras quilt on the short grass by the back door. We eat fat blueberries, lick barbecue sauce off our fingers, drink sparkling wine just for fun. And now we are in bed, this small ellipsis of time, with just us among the sheets; just our breathing, our sighs, our limbs loose under the covers.

Unable to stop myself I start in about tomorrow. You know I am someone who craves plans. In my head I make calculations, things lining up, the day sorted out just so. I like knowing what I can count on or expect.

You laugh. "Do we really have to talk about tomorrow?"

"I like to," I whisper back, my tongue running over my just-brushed teeth. "I like to plan."

You laugh and reach out. Just the slightest movement of your wrist. Enough, so that your hand touches the curve just above my hip. It's soft there, marked with the thin silver lines of newish stretch marks. Not many, but enough to show I twice birthed our long-eyelashed boys.

"I know you do," you say. "But I don't. I like to picture other things."

"What kinds of things?" It stuns me that after a decade together, we still have all these private uncharted places in our souls.

Outside the stars are bright and the sky is black. Things keep bumping into the screens. Things we cannot see, that buzz. What you say next is the most unexpected thing:

"I like to picture that I'm traveling through space." Your voice is soft, like you are already leaving. "Like I am going through galaxies."

And after a small pause you say, "Or I like to picture something that I've pictured since I was a kid."

I wait. "What?"

"That I'm on a mattress, sledding through endless snow." You laugh.

I smile, imagining you on your mattress amid an endless avalanche of white, the tips of pine trees zipping by. I can hardly comprehend how we have fallen asleep side by side for so many years, my skin pressed against yours, our breath becoming steady together, our dreams gathering close, and yet we have never talked about this, never shared the map of our clandestine exits from ourselves.

"What do you do?" you want to know.

"I sort of watch a slide show. A montage of images. Stuff from the day that breaks apart, one thing bumping into the next, until I'm seeing glimpses of stuff that I haven't thought about in years. Like right now, I just saw a snapshot of when I was sixteen, trying on a pair of jeans in a thrift store in Ohio. I ripped the metal PEPE tag off them and kept it, even though I didn't buy the jeans."

"Mmm," you grunt. Then laugh softly and pull me closer.

Here we are, every night leaving ourselves. Me, on a crash course with the visual riffraff that fills my head; you slipping and sliding toward stars, toward snow.

"I like to picture movement," you say.

I feel like a girl, like someone who has just fallen in love with this boy.

"I wish I could do that," I whisper, my nose now against your cheek. Me, the girl who has always wished she could dance.

Instead, sleep comes to me and the images behind my eyelids become unrelated and distilled, until they are just a gesture of a shoulder, a glance, a match being struck, a pottery bowl, a color.

You pull me even closer. Whisper, "You can come with me on my mattress in the snow."

And here I am, whirling down an endless embankment of snow that is not cold, under a sky that looks like a blue enamel bowl. Already I feel your rib cage begin to rise and fall with the slow tempo of sleep. Already you are dreaming.

• • •

The beginning of fall feels like running downhill. The days are a blur of leaves turning color, sap draining from the stem. If I listen, I can hear apples falling from the trees outside the window when my fingers pause from moving like a hailstorm across the keyboard.

You are downstairs, the boys underfoot so I can write.

"No! No, get down. What is it with you boys? That's enough of you. Go play with your toys!" you exclaim, irritated with their endless interruptions and chatter.

Then there is the clatter of pots and your words lift out the window to where the flickers and crows are calling the way such birds do. One abrupt remark, then silence. A communication with the wet leaves and the stippled shade, and with the other feathered hearts of similar birds, their dark wings folded, their claws holding tight to the damp branches.

Some days we can't help it. Our words intersect but never meet. Our conversations sound like a Salinger story, each line of dialogue left hanging, bifurcated like the V's of geese cutting through the air, my intentions going one way, yours another.

Today the sky is stormy.

By the pond in the morning I don't find the blue heron that stood all summer, balancing on one leg as it fished in the shallows. And on our dirt road, work crews have been preparing for winter. They bring loads of gravel and grade the worn surface until it is even and new.

Later, the wind will bring more round crabapples to the ground, and when we go for a walk together in the evening, we will startle the deer that have come to eat the wild fruit.

• • •

As you walk through the tall grass, your shoulders hunched, I sit inside at the table by the bowl of apples, trying to do other things. And in the dead maple a woodpecker knocks. I know we both hear it, though you said, "I want to be alone," and left, the screen door banging, walking away from me.

Now I climb the stairs to look for you out the window. I find you there, across the field, wearing orange, like a small flame. I've been there too; wandering through a field of dry grass and sorrow that makes my throat swell.

Everything could tip now. We both know this. But I keep feeling like there isn't anything we can do except kneel and give thanks. To pray as we listen to the woodpecker's rat-tat-tatting, and let it be the Morse code of our hearts.

• • •

We wake up and sing in the shower, or wake up and bury our heads. We wake up grinning, or we wake up feeling like shit. Sometimes we wake before the children and burrow into each other's warmth, lingering like otters; other times we wake late with heavy eyelids, and then the green numbers on the bedside clock become unforgiving marshals of lateness.

Whatever way we wake up, we move toward the day together. This is a thing we give each other daily, this small act in tandem, this slight choreography of promise between us—the way a leaf always flutters in response to the wind. And so the day starts in again.

We pull on jeans and pull apart the tussle under way on our bed: two boys in various states of undress. We pull off pajamas, pull on T-shirts, diapers, underwear, socks. We make coffee. Pour cereal. Scramble eggs. We hold hands. We hold the hands of our boys. We hold hats and jackets and empty half-gallon milk jars to be returned to the farm. We hold half-eaten raspberry jam toast, more coffee in to-go mugs, wallets, keys. We hold our breath. We hold each other.

• • •

There was frost this morning. Gossamer. The ghost of winter already creeping in among the still-green clover and hip-high grass. Autumn, when the monarchs leave our milkweed fields, is really here. Prussian skies. The harsh calling of geese. Water, low in the creeks, reflecting the first flame-flecked leaves of the maples up to the sky. The grass is ruffled with wind.

I am lying in the field above the hill behind our house, all alone. I close my eyes and let go, feeling the earth spin. I can feel the way my cells are drinking in this solitude, replenishing the part of me that has grown sparse in the past few months, when every moment was jam-packed with responsibility for things that had very much to do with us, but rarely with just me.

I know you feel this too, this fierce need for time spent alone, all day doing things according to pure selfish whimsy. We both thirst for it, just as we thirst for each other, and this is the push and pull

I think we'll always feel. A struggle to reconcile our separate selves with the sum of all our love.

I look up to see a fighter jet tear through the overcast sky; no contrail, no sound, and then the sudden sonic thunder that follows after, the plane already a distant arrow moving across a cloud-torn sky full of geese and crows. I think of the pilot up there, his solitary heart also full of thunder, and every day I am stunned by this anew: that we are all here, breathing.

All of us, with ribs and drawers of dreams and latched container hearts, beating secretively while we occupy our lives with the things we make and the things we do: motors and binary code, spreadsheets and arguments. Tenderness, dinner. Promises, made or broken. Some things fall apart while others hold: a seam, a paper flour sack, an origami kite, a heart, a life we have together.

It's easy, from the outside, to imagine things are perfect in everyone else's life, easy to varnish Hollywood's happy ending over it all. But what I want to tell you is this: that love is the mess. That joy is finding this love again and again at the eye of the storm. That happiness is in the give-and-take.

Field Notes:
INTERSECTION

intersection |in tər ˈsek shən| (n.):
a common point at which two or more things
meet, cross, or intersect.

Love, like any other
remarkable thing, requires
intention every day, and
it's vital to cultivate certain
guidelines that will hold in the heat of the
moment when things derail.

These are ours: Curiosity. Interest. A
promise to never intentionally hurt each
other, and a commitment to keep showing
up when the moments matter, at this
intersection between us.

What guidelines can you make to sustain
you?

Meadowlark. *Sturnella magna*
Western Meadowlark. *Sturnella magna*

CONTENTS

Off Track: Journey

There are a hundred things on my to-do list, and not one of them is taking a walk with my eldest son. Yet right now it is the only thing that I can do. He's been dogging me for the past half-hour, his questions becoming increasingly persistent.

"Mama, do you have Post-it notes? Mama, do you know about thunder sharks? Mama, look! Mama! Mama?"

There is something about the resistance of the moment. There comes a point when persisting in whatever I am doing results in an inevitably bad outcome, a meltdown, jelly legs, little hands curled into fists, and so I take his hand and follow his lead, and let my work hang in suspended animation.

I bring my camera, hoping for something unfamiliar, though I know nearly every rut and mailbox and tree by heart after three years of living in this place. But today it's easier than I expect: Liam darts off into the uncharted landscape of a neighbor's field and I follow after.

The field is wide, and the snow deep, grass poking through it brown and folded, like the limbs of long-legged birds. Liam dashes ahead, then stops abruptly and squats down to look at something in the snow. My shadow overtakes him. I hold my breath as I come up beside him, watching as his breath lifts like a cloud in the cold air above his head.

From here our house looks small and perched, like a storybook cottage up on the hill, white, and gabled, and distant; and for a moment I am astounded by the way our legs have carried us all the way here, where the tracks of voles and field mice make fidgety paths across the snow between tall patches of grass, and the fat blue shadow of a solitary wooden fence post marks the path of the noon-time sun above us.

Together we look toward the woods below us, toward a place we've never gone, on property that is not ours. It looks abrupt and dark against the snow, with a row of pointed pines just visible over the slope of the field, and when I glance down at my feet I can see now that we've been standing on coyote tracks. They must come up from the woods, crossing this field at dusk, tongues lolling, breath rising in frothy clouds from their mouths.

We hear them often in the night. Their wild yelping makes the hair on my neck rise, even as I am always compelled to go to the nearest window and fling it open to listen, despite the cold. You can hear them moving: nearer, nearer up the frozen creek bed, until they are just beyond the edge of the porch light, the moon a grinning wedge above the trees. And then they're gone, racing up the valley into the dark.

I can feel how they're close now, beyond the meadow's edge, somewhere in the woods there, maybe asleep or watching us with yellow eyes, alerted by our footsteps and the sharp, ringing singsong of my son's eager voice.

This is always the case: The line between us and the wild is slender, like the bit of thread I find coiled in my pocket. My fingers tease it, wanting to know how it's wound. This is always the way. I always want to know. The thread is yellow and snarled and comes from the windowsill of the bedroom above the garage. I stuck it in my pocket this morning while tidying, meaning to throw it away.

It was from tha same window that I saw the foxes last week. The ruckus of the chickens alerted me, and when I looked down, one was right below me in the snowy driveway, looking up. I pounded my fist on the glass and began to yell, but it didn't run.

Instead it just stared at me, not moving a muscle until I ran down and out into the snow without a hat or gloves or jacket, boots unlaced, shrieking like a mad-woman. Of course it ran then, though not far at first—just to the top of the nearest field—and when I followed after, another joined it. They'd staked the chicken house out for sure.

And even though they were a threat to our unwitting hens, I was sad when they disap-peared among the white trunks of a stand of birches, and I can still feel the way my heart was hammering hard and raw in my chest after running through the snow, hair flyaway, clapping my hands. Their fur was rust-colored, and when they ran they became streaks of umber, like flaming contrails in a dream. So beautiful, I wanted to cry.

It's the same feeling I have now, and my eyes well up as I bend down with my son to examine other marks in the snow where something struggled. Wing marks maybe, in broken spirals. This is what noticing always does: It fills me with wonder, and forces me beyond the ease of being unaffected by the world.

I put the thread back into my pocket and exhale softly. Together we walk back toward the road over the windblown snow, following the zigzag tracks we made before. The air is still and cold. The sky is pale and filled with cirrus, and along the road starlings sit on telephone wires calling to one another, lifting and alighting in unison. Down the way two men are working on a silo, and their tools make hard metallic sounds that travel to us across the distance. *Clink. Clink. Clink.*

I want to hold on to this. To this wildness. To this stillness. I know it is the thing I need the most, especially when I pick up the work I've left unfinished, and return to the rush of all the things that I must do.

It takes veering off course to remember that I am an animal first. That in my bones and blood and breath is a wildness that is sustained with wonder; that my creative well doesn't fill when I stand over it, pouring myself in, on task, on target, up late every night without ceasing.

It takes tracks in the snow to remember: Creativity is an energy that tumbles through you in a torrent, like a snowmelt creek or the coyote's song. It's a substance of the immediate present, a thing that doesn't adhere to the traditional rules of work. Put more in to get more out. It's not a thing that blooms wildly from a box of regular hours.

Instead it's about this: My most important work often begins when I'm not working. Creativity wells up when I give myself the present. When I go with eyes wide under open skies and allow the world to split me open.

The more you open yourself like this, the more you give yourself to the rawness of world, outdoors and uncharted, the more your work will work for you. It's a game of unlikely cause and effect where the whole universe plays along.

See for yourself. Interrupt your work for a short while. Leave your house or your office or your car. Maybe take your camera, or a notebook, or your dog pulling at its leash, or your child who will want to go at irregular speeds, first dashing boldly, then slowing almost to a stop.

Field Notes:
JOURNEY

journey | ˈjər nē| (n.):
travel from one place to another,
usually taking a long time; a pas-
sage or progress from one stage
to another.

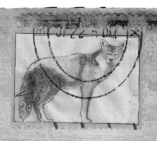

Be ready for what you don't expect to see. Veer
off the path. Hesitate. Linger. Or run till your lungs
feel raw. Make up a challenge: Find six round stones,
maybe, or a view you've never seen. Stalk wonder.
Pay attention to your legs and lungs and breath:
how together they have moved you to wherever you
are, each capillary thundering in minute harmony,
each muscle bunchy and sure beneath your jeans,
beneath your skin.
                    under your footsteps . . . .
Go back only when you have been altered by wonder.

At Home in the Moment:
Listing

Spring sounds like the robin here, and when its song lifts from the tree above me it feels like helium is being pumped into my lungs, like I might just lift off the ground with the notes of its tremulous vermilion song.

I cannot help feeling the precarious tilt of things now: the way everything turns green with spring; the way life starts, deepens, deepens. Below my feet I imagine the nematodes and newts still hibernating in quiet coils below last season's decomposing leaves. Like me, they are waiting for sun to quicken their brief lives. And from the perch I've found along the rock wall between field and woods, I feel how my life is tethered only briefly to this earth, to this new grass and trillium and maples turning red.

I used to think that living an extraordinary life meant living like my grandmother once did, before the rest of her life began, when she spent six months traveling around the world with my grandfather just after they were married. I used to think a remarkable life must be exotic, not

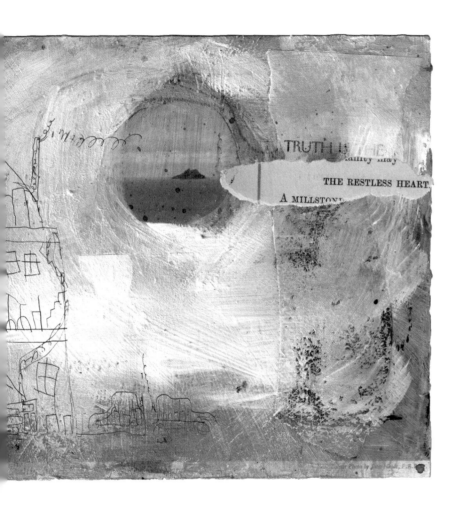

TRUTH IS THE
ranity may
THE RESTLESS HEART
A MILLSTONE

one rooted with young children among fields and old stone walls. I would never have imagined for a second how it could be this: the work of gathering moments in a place.

I can remember being sixteen, eighteen, twenty-four, and proclaiming, "My greatest goal in life is to live without regret." I was too young then to have any idea what regret could really mean, but for the longest time it was both a mantra and a kind of secret fear. I was compelled, driven, and anxious with every choice I made: Was this life I was living the right one?

I still believed this when Todd and I moved into a small beachside bungalow with a yellow dog. It was our second place three years into our life together. Sometimes the tides would come all the way up the street and a siren would sound and everyone would come out of their houses and find their cars and drive them up to higher ground, to garages or side streets, and then the water would come rushing in, licking over the seawall, and filling the street with debris.

I was teaching at a charter school then. Todd was working for one of the decade's big day-trading firms that has since gone belly-up. We had a big TV, a fast little car, and a beach with endless pebbles to claim. Still, I wondered.

When we came back from staying at a lakeside cabin in Vermont the weekend he proposed and I said yes, we found our house had been infested with fleas. I was unpacking bags in the laundry room when I discovered it. I bent down to pick up an armload of rumpled towels and bathing suits, and dozens of them sprang onto my legs. We thought it was hilarious and also mortifying, and drove together to the store for a couple of those terribly toxic flea-bomb canisters, set them off, and drove away again, staying somewhere else for another night.

But the truth is, things could have just as easily fallen apart between us that day and I wouldn't have been surprised. Picking up and moving on still mostly meant throwing a couple pairs of jeans into a bag with my pen and notebook—and I still believed that living well meant staying in motion and keeping my options open. It was the summer after my father died. I was twenty-five, with restless blood churning in my veins. I expected, maybe, to marry Todd. I also expected that I might not. I expected needing to leave on a moment's notice, the minute the tide turned.

What I didn't expect was the way my heart would gradually settle into a love that was vastly beyond the tinsel strength of that early affection, or that I would locate my calling here, grounded in this life of fields and rainstorms and boys.

Now, returning from my walk to the old, stone wall, I find Todd prepping for dinner in the kitchen. He is scrubbing a pan in the sink when I come in. His muscles ripple under the blue fabric of his shirt as he turns, dries the pan with a faded red-and-white towel, and puts it on the stove. Then he drizzles in a little olive oil and turns the gas flame on. There is certainty and comfort in the way he smiles when he looks up to see me watching, and in the way I join then, peeling garlic and rinsing arugula, in the routine preparing dinner.

• • •

Still, I come from a long line of restless women.

When my grandmother fell in love with her cousin and was forbidden to marry him, she left for Europe on an ocean liner. She met my grandfather on that voyage, a German farmer who was also leaving behind an unrequited love. They played tag on the boat's deck. Crossed the ocean. Returned. And a year later they were married.

There is such optimism and delight on her face in the photos I have of her then. In one, she is standing by a steamer trunk, poised for their honeymoon trip around the world, just four months after they were married. She is wearing a beret and a sly grin, undeterred by impossibly slim savings, the Depression, and relatives shaking their heads. But when they returned nine months later, they settled in to lead lives that were more expected: My grandfather got a job as a farm machinery and fertilizer salesman, and my grandmother got pregnant with the first of their four children. Once he could afford it, my grandfather bought a dairy farm in the Pennsylvania country-side, and my grandmother became simply a farmer's wife.

I imagine her at her kitchen window, looking out at the red dairy barns nestled in the rolling Appalachian hills, restless with what her life offered: three boys and a little girl, arguments, family dinners, Persian carpets growing threadbare with use. She wore stockings and peacoats when trousers would have been more practical; drank tea in the afternoon from a china cup; wrote hundreds of sonnets. Maybe what she wanted was heady conversation, or city life; Shakespeare and Goethe, opera, a sense of daring. Or maybe all she wanted was for someone to recognize how much it mattered that she listened to Beethoven while ironing shirts instead of to the radio. I am not certain of any of these things. All I know is that before she died, she burned all but a handful of the sonnets that she wrote.

My mother, too, settled again and again for the life my father chose. In the beginning she left Pennsylvania to live with him in a log cabin high in the broken bowl of the Rocky Mountains, where she hung my cloth diapers to dry in subzero temperatures in winter, and then carried them indoors, flat as boards, to thaw by the woodstove. Next she moved with him to an angular little house on a hill among flammable eucalyptus in the Los Angeles suburbs, where the Santa Ana winds made the carpets ripple, and smoke from wildfires obscured the San Bernardino Mountains in the summer.

Eventually she moved with him again, to a low ranch with tacky floral wallpaper on a winding macadam road in Northern California, where the grass was green in January and dead by May. It was there, where the farmers would spray yellow clouds of pesticides onto the vineyards in the spring, that my father died of pancreatic cancer, leaving my mother's restless heart unmoored. Right off, she sold the house. Then she dashed off, grief painting her days the color of smashed grapes, and she rented one house after the next, moving from zip code to zip code with a certain unnamed restlessness and longing for home—feelings she'd always ascribed to my father.

Somehow I memorized the message: *Settling* always meant settling for something, and likely, something less. And for years I believed that if I put down roots and grew a family I would become like my mother and her mother before her: restless with regret for a life they never had or could never quite imagine.

And so I spent years perfecting the art of recklessness: I climbed water towers with boys, trespassed, hitchhiked, went skinny-dipping at night—as though momentum were the only way to live without regret. But what I know now is that regret is always possible, even when you try to run between the raindrops. On many days the moments of your life will simply devour you and spit you out carelessly, the pit of something new.

But there is also this: When I woke this morning I had a head-ache, and wanted to cry, but now the kitchen window is open just a little and the air rushing in is sweet with rain and new leaves and the first blossoms, and if joy had a scent it would be this. Rain-drenched, fragrant, and stirring with birdsong.

When we came here four years ago with a six-month-old, gut-ted this house, and put in tile and soapstone and maple with our own hands, we learned a hundred lessons about how to be alive at the very eye of the storm that all big dreams are. We showed up, half asleep in our lives, and were shaken awake by seasons, and work, and wildness. I've learned the vireo's call, and have been marked by the purple martin's swooping flight over the pond. I've planted roses and tomatoes, stacked wood, weathered storms, grown steadier in my center. Now when we move about the kitchen, our actions are synchronized around the boys giggling at our feet. I crush garlic in a wooden bowl; he marinates chicken in yogurt and thyme.

This is the difference: I've chosen this life. And even on the spiteful days, when I can only look at the unfolded heaps of laundry or at the way the food scraps cling to the strainer in the sink, I know this: Everything can always be one way, and then another. The pres-ent is always unfolding. Every day is a small surprise. Being alive is fickle and brief, each day a handful of moments like pebbles bump-ing against each other in God's pockets. The mountains are blue. The day blooms. Clouds come. They bring rain. These are all possibilities.

The difference between restlessness and regret is this: The moment always offers a choice. The very fact that I can make this life, that I can write myself into any future I imagine, listing my longing and moving toward it, is because before me there were women who put their dreams on hold, believing they never had the choice to take them up. Regret is not my inheritance; choice is. And with it my heart can always be a satellite, a parachute, a thing capable of flight.

Now as I watch a flock of dark-winged birds alight in the branches of the red maple out the kitchen window, though I do not know what they are called, I think I know what they must feel as they lift again in unison and circle above the house in a sudden stirring of air.

Listlessness is an incredibly literal state of affairs if you think about it, and when I begin to feel wanderlust spreading through me like a fever as the world turns green, I make a list of real intentions.

Just like that, what you list for, you can move toward. It is no wonder that to list is also a verb. Lists are a flirtation between the present and the future. They are an antidote to restlessness, a balm for spring fever.

Once when I was stung by a honeybee as a child, my grandmother mixed sugar and water into a paste and applied it to my arm, telling me the sweetness would draw out the sting. I am not sure now if this actually does work, but I remember the promise that she made, and that it worked. The stinging stopped, and I think this is the secret. Our minds are beehives of wonder and capacity.

There is enormous power in putting into words the things you long for. I believe this with every single cell in my being. Even when what we ask for is far greater than what we're capable of manifesting ourselves. When your intention is clear, the universe moves too. The difficult thing on some days is believing that it will. But we do spend our whole life on a planet that spins. Does that ever startle you?

It takes guts and nerve and passion to lean toward your longing. But mostly, it takes imagination. It is easy to feel like nothing will ever amount from the small moments of your life. It will.

Your right life is happening. Zero in. Let the things you long for come into focus; things you can hardly imagine. List them.

This has nothing to do with changing your circumstances, or your bank account, or your love life, right this minute. It has to do with being right here and choosing.

What matters is listing with intention.

ANCO

I always write a list of things to accomplish before my next birthday—thirty-two things before I am thirty-two, thirty-three before thirty-three—and each year I look back, surprised by how many have come to fruition. Even the most outrageous things—even ones that feel too big and impossible to hope for—when put there on the page become a kind of invitation for the universe to play along.

Field Notes:
LISTING

listing | 'lis ting | (v.):
to want; to like or desire; to wish; choose.

For the Time Being:
Measure

For weeks I have been watching an elderly couple at a cafe I frequent to write. The man is dying slowly, his hands growing frail, and the woman is waiting for all the unknown ways her life will change. Today I order a double latte with whole milk and then sit down to write. They are at the table across the room, and now I watch as she rises to get more cream. She brings it to him, then puts her hands on his shoulders and hesitates there.

I see her look away.

Today there is this: What we have ends, begins, ends again, always. And when it's over, all that we have becomes a fragile calliope of winding song, a promise, a thin silver thread connecting us to the other side. How we pray doesn't matter. Kneeling doesn't matter. Pressing palms together doesn't matter. What matters is the way the trees have lost their leaves now and stand stark and surprised, yet their stilling sap continues to hold the memory of bud, of newly furling leaf, of quivering branch lifting toward the sky.

Why do we hesitate at the doorway of our hearts, becoming distracted with the frail shells of things like impatience, worry, anxiety, stress?

I caught myself this morning, waiting for my glass to fill. I could feel impatience rising almost immediately in the length of time it took for the cool, filtered water from the refrigerator to spill into my glass.

So long, imagine that. I counted the seconds: one, two, three, four, five, six, seven, eight.

How is it possible that in eight seconds I already had the urge to move along; that I let impatience seep in, even in this brief scrap of time, standing in the kitchen, waiting for water to drink?

Why the rush?

So what that the glass took eight seconds to fill? So what if it took twenty? The floor was lit with the bright geometry of sun and angles. Outside the mountains were the color of blue chalk. I was so eager for what? For eight more seconds of uninterrupted time while the baby slept? For eight more seconds to get things done?

When I look at the couple again, it is just in time to see the man point to the bulletin board by the door, awkwardly knocking the sugar on its side as he does, and she responds, gathering the sweetness with a napkin. Brushing the grains into the trash. Then they are leaving.

Today she goes ahead of him, pressing her fingers to her lips. He follows after, a newspaper folded under his arm. She walks out the door first, her long gray hair blowing into her face as a truck barrels past. I watch out the window as she turns back toward the door. At first her face is carelessly at ease, but then she looks at him and her features soften almost imperceptibly with resignation. He has paused on the landing, readying himself to tackle descending the stairs.

His hands have the same sparrow-like grasp and yellow skin my father had when he was in the throes of pancreatic cancer. The same hunched shoulders in a flannel shirt. The same slow, deliberate effort to carry on with the minutia of the day. Coffee in a paper cup; the laces of his leather boots tied in double knots. These things mean different things in the end.

The man holds the metal rail and takes each step, one at a time. Then he puts his palm on her shoulder and they turn and go.

It is maybe reasonable to say that we have more time now since we have invented machines to do the work we used to do. But what are we doing with all the time and ease we've gained, as our lives become easier and faster every second? Now that we no longer need to scrub our shirts or write letters by hand, or walk to the general store for flour, coffee, and gossip, how are we using those precious minutes saved? The truth is, we fill most days as quickly as possible—as though the world won't wait if we go slowly; as though there isn't time to simply be right here with reverie and focus.

• • •

Later, I am giving my son a haircut. He is sitting bare-chested on the stool in front of me, looking anywhere but up, and every few seconds he squirms, his small body barraged with itches. On his bare shoulders are the snippets from too-long bangs, and I am trying to make even cuts, but the whole thing is taking much longer than it should because each time he wriggles, I have to pull the scissors back and wait for him to settle, impatience swarming like mosquitoes. I want to yell at him, *Sit still already!*

But then I think about way the man in the cafe moved—slowly, persisting in the simple tasks of living—and the way the woman offered her attention and patience and her unguarded heart to simply being there with him, drinking coffee.

And so I tell my son a story about Mr. Mole and his old-fashioned sidecar motorcycle. I whisper, "Close your eyes," and then blow the stray bits of hair like dandelion fluff from his cheeks and squinched eyelashes and thin shoulders. I breathe in and then out slowly when I feel irritation prickle, as he squirms again and again, the scissors nicking close.

Fidgeting on the stool in front of me is a boy with a head full of ideas and peculiarities. My eldest son. Yet in this instant I am suddenly aware that he is already staking his claim on the world; marking his own way, shedding my concern, my hopes, my rebukes. His hair falls to the floor, ashy and blond, like chaff, like summer grass.

This is what I know: The heart is not a machine. It does not have the capacity to love at any greater speed, or to feel anything more deeply, when the pace is doubled. While fast is better for machines, we're fools to live by such a rule set every day. Rushing every second, we forget that we're capable of a certain quality of joy that can be arrived at only slowly, as time unfolds.

• • •

The next time I am at the cafe, the light is almost unbearably golden, slanting across the ecru walls and coffee cups and wide plank floors. This time the couple is seated at the table next to the one I claim. It occurs to me that they must come even on the mornings that I do not, and I like the thought of this constant that remains for them, for the time being.

They've been here a while, their plates already empty. I can't help watching as she fixes her long hair, then wipes the crumbs from the table and leans back patiently.

After a while she says, "Shall we?"

He nods.

"Are you going to drink the rest of your coffee?" she asks then, standing, gathering the plates with the croissant crumbs and the wooden stir stick, broken in two parts. The broken ends are sharp.

"Yes, I might." He reaches for his cup, holding it possessively as she clears.

She smiles and puts the dishes in the bin, then walks back to him, rests her hand on the back of his neck. Waits. Today he doesn't want to leave. He avoids her eyes and looks out the window instead, so she sits again, and watches him.

"Well," he says, and the word just hovers in the air softly, like a cat pacing back and forth between them.

For him, conversation is less important now. Just being here is something. Here in this room with people's voices rising and falling, and the rush of cold air as others open the door, order warm drinks, sit, laugh. He is thinner than last time. His ring—a thick band that matches hers—hangs loosely around his finger. He turns his head to look out the window and the sun illuminates his face.

"All right," she says finally. "Two more minutes, and then we really do have to go."

As she waits, she points things out to him: the man who walks past the cafe windows wearing a bright red scarf and heavy black boots. The way the house across the street has reused old cardboard boxes to gather up their leaves. They know people here, but when a couple stops to say hello, he gives her a questioning look. Patiently, matter-of-factly, she reminds him who they are.

Then she says, "Okay," and puts her coat on. "All right, let's go."

She puts her hand out but he doesn't take it. Instead he stands slowly. So slowly.

His belt is too large, and he clumsily begins to unbuckle it to make it tighter, his fingers fumbling. And just like that, she reaches to help him. Right there in the middle of the room, she unbuckles it, and cinches it tighter. Then she tries to help him with his gloves, but he takes them from her.

Then he slowly puts them on his hands himself.

It takes a long time for him to get down the stairs today, and

I think how eventually there will come a time when stairs will no longer be possible. A time when they will stop coming.

But it's not today. Today she puts her sunglasses on, and then she turns to him and nods.

The moments arrive, then leave us, one by one.

I check the time and realize I'm running late to pick up my son at Pre-K. I shove things hastily into my bag, and at my car, I fumble for the keys, searching every pocket of my bag. I do this always. It seems like such a simple act to put keys where I will find them, but each day it is the same. I've already moved on in my mind, skipping past *right now*. I bite my lip in consternation. I vow to do better, to slow down, to be right here.

And this is what I am thinking about, driving toward Liam's school, the music turned off for once, the windows rolled down so I can feel the cold winter air. Then up at the stoplight where I'm supposed to turn, there are lights flashing, red and white, and my heart leaps up, an unquiet fish in my chest.

Traffic crawls, then stops. I will be late. Still, there is no choice now but to be right here, waiting, with certain crumpled metal up ahead.

An ambulance passes, then a fire truck. On a stretcher, someone. I whisper hope into the air, fragrant with exhaust and doughnuts being made at the bakery across the street. And then I wait for someone to direct me around the smashed cars, folded one into the other. Briefly, my day becomes snarled like a burr in the weft of these moments here that will define for someone how things will always be different.

But soon a man with a reflective vest and day-old stubble waves me on, and behind me, another ambulance pulls into the space where my car idled, the air invariably still warm with exhaust. I go.

• • •

Somehow, months have fled past, and though winter is still throwing its bucket of whitewash at the world, everything is on the verge of spring. I can feel it in the air today, the way things are changing. There is steam rising from every sugarhouse, and all the back roads have turned to mud. I'm restless, feeling the way I do when I don't make enough time for the work that matters to me most: words on the page.

And so I do something I am not particularly good at: I ask for help. I am not sure why it is so hard to accept that this life and work aren't things we can do alone, but it has something to do with the way we believe that what we do ourselves indicates some kind of circumference around the things we can control. It's an illusion, of course, and when I ask, my in-laws come with open arms to babysit my youngest son while I go eagerly to the cafe with a new Moleskine notebook, to write.

I arrive at about the same time I am usually there, and scan the room, knowing immediately they are not here. They haven't been for weeks now, or at least, not when I am. It's possible, of course, that they've just changed their schedule and arrive and leave at other times, and I almost ask at the counter. It's a small place. They'd probably know.

But what would I do then? Stand here with my lemon scone, with sudden tears running down my cheeks?

I could see it, last time, when watching him leave slowly made everything in me ache. There was still snow then. Now the sun is supple and there is plenty of it, and in a week we set our clocks forward and chlorophyll will return to the trampled lawns. Sap is running, and I imagine in the man's veins a slow, reluctant blood.

Likely hospice volunteers come now to change the sheets on his hospital-issue bed, and she is there, spending nights beside him, mornings, days, watching the light move across his room; trying to be brave. Trying to smile when he looks around for her, disoriented (morphine will do this) in a maze of the present that continues to be his life. And still it's likely he won't let go for a little while longer. I imagine this is so because of the way he shook her off, last time I saw them leaving, with a little impatient flick of an elbow as he made his way toward the door.

So she went first, opening it, then letting it swing closed, so that he could open it again—something so incidental, yet so important. Leaving is everything for him now, and he doesn't want to go at all. How many times we open doors, shut them, arrive effortlessly, leave; rushing always and imagining we are in control. By summer he'll have lifted off and she'll be left with her long gray hair and the soft curves of her body and her round cheeks.

• • •

On the way to the cafe this morning, I called my sister. She is pregnant, and today she said, "I'm just tired of sharing my space, of having everything I do affect someone else all the time." As though this will end when she gives birth.

We all have illusions about the way things will begin or end. We keep expecting things to even out; keep imagining there will be smoother waters up ahead. Less to do, more time to go back and read what we've bookmarked, make amends, say what we mean, eat well, exercise, make love. We imagine more time, brighter options, better connections, easier odds.

It's easy to get caught up in rushing toward the future in this way. But the truth is, the future doesn't hold. I was twenty-four when my father died and my life was like an ink blot, blurry and startling.

I had no idea what was happening then—what this loss meant, how my life would be. And maybe this is always the way it is: You cannot know how the moments shape you when you're in them. Perspective comes only after, when loss becomes a lens.

Now, through the viewfinder of my own life, I see the empty chairs at the cafe table where the couple often sat. And on the way back home, with coffee still warm at the bottom of my paper cup, I pass the remains of a mink at the side of the road, dark-furred, its face unmarred, its body squished through the middle. I'm always sort of shocked by the red guts of animals that get spilled this way along the road—that they stay red, and stain the pavement and the snow for a while. It makes me sad. It makes me want to pray. It makes me wish there was another way to be here.

But life keeps on, and dying too. This is the cost of living: We are only briefly here, on this fecund planet that is always blooming and decaying as seconds turn to rust.

In quiet white-walled laboratories, there are scientists who spend their days keeping track of time. They spin atoms into exquisitely precise clocks that do not lose or gain a second for 200 million years—a fact they test by speeding up the ticking of the clock to 430 trillion ticks per second. Yet they have not found a single way to slow things down. But if you could—if you could have another hour, clean like an empty plate, like a crescent moon, like a promise—what would you use it for?

Answer this now, in the margins here, or on whatever scrap of paper is at hand: If you could really have an hour more, what would you do?

For me, many days the honest answer would be sleep. I stumble through my days with too little, too often. Other times, it would simply be having a little time to myself. Rest and solitude are

If you are really serious about doing whatever you've just written down, make the time. Ask yourself: What can you let fall by the wayside for a while? The laundry always can. So can e-mail, or saying yes when what you really mean is no.

Then, ask for help, even if it feels hard to do—especially then. We all need each other.

There is a certain grace in accepting attention, kindness, and care, just as there is grace in giving it.

absolutely vital to my creative work. This is not new or radical; it is real, and personal and urgent. This is about making time for moments that fill you, about the wind moving among thousands of apple-tree leaves, and it is about the mystery of how each apple—with seeds like a star inside its sweet, ripe fruit—began with the gift of the honeybee, bringing pollen from flower to flower.

Field Notes:
MEASURE

measure | ˈme zhər| (v.): to estimate or assess the extent, quality, value, or effect of something; (n.) a plan or course of action taken to achieve a particular purpose.

Certain Uncertainty:
Opportunity

It begins with rain falling softly, then harder, signaling the start of a season; with the smallness of a single step; with a breath, a reaction. Then we're in the thick of it, waiting, our entire lives up for grabs. Waiting for news, a phone call, an outcome, a best-case scenario—a job offer.

This is what I know: On Christmas Island, north of Australia, crabs crawl to the sea each monsoon season, their carapaces red and round, enclosing their gills and guts and a certain unwavering instinct that calls them back to the shore again and again. They do not know of hope, or promise, or peril. They do not waver, or consider what else they might do. They only know that when the rains start, something calls them from their sheltered burrows in the forests, and inside their crushable bodies another thing replies, forcing a sideways scuttle toward the shore to breed and lay their eggs.

For us it begins when the leaves are new and the ground is still soft; with a decision, a declaration, his, after an entire year of loss in the stock

MISCELLA

F SUNS

Su

and hamlets
us and vapo
ossel with
he landscape

and B Equal Day and Night; E Longest Da
E Shortest Day.
ich the sun is furthe
th or south

AUTUMNAL
EQUINOX
SEPT. 23.

WINTER
SOLSTICE
DEC. 23.

SUMMER
SOLSTICE
JUNE 2

VERNAL
EQUINOX
MARCH 20

E

A

market. His job has become so overwrought with risk and stress, every single day has become about being chin-up and making it through for all of us. We are standing in the living room when he tells me, and the early evening light makes everything golden in the room.

And even though they are words I've wanted him to say for so long, I can taste the fear in my mouth when he finally does. Fear of what might happen; of all the ways that we could fail; of everything I can't control.

"I'm quitting finally."

Such small words.

• • •

And now the leaves are thick and green and the light lasts late past the children's bedtime. The grass grows and grows and begs to be mowed once a week, twice, and I've gradually come to understand that I must exhale into not knowing.

He's applied, interviewed, and interviewed again. The waiting now is like a slow and inevitable migration. Each day we begin, carry on, eat, sleep, and wonder. Each day we know what we do not know, and this rubs like a blister, like the bit of sand at the heart of a pearl. This is the risk: If the phone doesn't ring, everything could be crushed in the ensuing landslide of figuring things out anew. We could lose our house, perhaps, or worse, our sense of who we are. Simply, if the phone never rings, we'll have to wade out again, risking more, feeling more, the accumulated weight of this uncertainty bearing down upon us like a thundering tide.

During migration the crabs on Christmas Island can be seen from the air, a river of red exoskeletons, crushed by cars, by trains, by bicycles, by unseeing feet. They move inevitably along the paths they have always followed toward the sea, crossing walkways, roadways, grass, risking everything for an outcome they have no capacity to understand. This is the risk: Exposed on dry land too long, the red crab's body will dry out and it will perish; but in water too deep it will drown, having lost its ancestral ability to swim. Still, its larvae remember, and it's only there that they can survive, rocked in the salty surf.

When the crabs reach the shore the males dig burrows, mate, and then return the way they came, but the females stay on, growing their eggs until they are ready to be released, precisely at the turn of the high tide during the last quarter of the moon. It's then that the water level is most constant for the greatest length of time. It's then they risk the least as they wade out into the surf, claws waving at the sky, and release their eggs that hatch immediately upon contact with the sea.

Today I crave such certain risks, such obvious results. As the day unravels without any, I begin to see how the things I can control are utterly quantifiable and small: the way I touch my baby's cheek, or the way I choose to avoid slinging raw-edged words back and forth with my husband out of fear. By afternoon I understand how insignificant I really am: speck-of-dust minute among the planets and the gods, and when I take a walk in the damp woods, I know that I am the only one who startles when an owl takes flight above my head.

When I return I sit at the kitchen table with a glass of ice water and an unfinished essay. Heat prickles on my skin as I reread it. Sweat spreads between my shirt and the chair, and across the room

I can see the thermometer continue to climb; 87 degrees, 89. The humidity is just as high, and already there is condensation on my glass. I have a handful of minutes now, a half-hour maybe while the boys are napping. Yet I am mired in the waiting. Without knowing the outcome of his job search, it feels impossible to dig in and commit to my own work.

My mind whirs: *What good will anything be anyway, if things come undone?* Limbo snares my thoughts like a handful of burrs, and this is what I do instead: I Google a classmate from college who has all the right connections, no children, and apparently ample certainty in her life. Her smile on her book jacket is like a cat having just eaten cream. I almost allow myself to mire here, immersed in self-pity and doubt. But then a bright streak flashes past the window: an oriole in the crab apple, so scandalously orange among the leaves, I cannot help but grin. Maybe we are held by these moments, by the specific uncertainties of our lives in the same way the red crabs are called to the sea when the rain falls. Or maybe not. Things are rarely as simple as they appear on the surface. In every life there is turbulence, just as there are always bright sparks of joy.

This is what I know: In the fields beside the road the corn flutters waist-high now. In the night the raccoons come, curious, raiding, their eyes a mask of delight. The days are filled with dreamy light. Summer is here regardless of my plight of wondering, and upstairs, sleeping, is my baby. His hair smells of lemon shampoo and pizza, and on the couch, also napping, is his brother, my firstborn, who sleeps with heavy eyelashes and pale lids, his breath coming quickly.

And here it is. This day, this table with the circles from my dripping glass, this slowly unfolding now is all I need. Without anything new, without any answers gleaned, or outcomes gained, this life holds something precious that calls me back again and again to this moment that I have. And it's this truth that thrums like the monsoon rains in my ears as I spend the heat of the humid afternoon circling the small parameters of my house, doing the smallest of domestic things, and waiting for the phone to ring with news.

It is inevitable: Your mind will buck about, confronted with the limbo of waiting. It will become restless, obsessive, distracted. It will leap ahead, imagining a hundred things—worst-case scenarios, wrong turns, missed chances.

Days later the phone does ring. I can't bear to stay and listen. He's worked so hard for this, for starting new, for sinking into work he really loves, and I can't stand the thought that it might be dire, and so I go instead with a bucket and rollers to paint the bedroom I've claimed as my studio. I turn the music up and pour the paint with voracious attention. Unwrap a roller, and then begin to cover the wall with reverence, and urgency, and absolute focus. Sweat makes the tendrils of hair around my face curl, and even with the windows open the humid air is heavy with the scent of new paint. I'm singing at the top of my lungs when Todd shows up at the doorway, grinning. He got the offer he wanted the most, in a field he loves, and when he picks me up and spins me around the room, laughing, I cry with relief.

And over the next few weeks I begin to wonder what it might be like to trust this life a little more—to see things not as possible wrong turns or missed chances, but choices and progress and possibility. For this is the truth: Life fills again and again with opportunity.

Field Notes:
OPPORTUNITY

opportunity |ä pər 'tü nə tē|
(n.):
a set of circumstances that
makes it possible to do
something; something occurring
at a favorable or useful time.

When you have nowhere else to be, nothing more urgent to do than waiting, try rinsing the dishes as though each plate and jammy knife bears a secret message: Right now is everything. Instead of becoming engulfed in what you cannot imagine, let your mind fill with concentric circles of attention, like the ripples that spread on the surface of a pond when you toss a pebble in. Let your focus be on the legs of the blue egret, and on the flat, sharp leaves of the cattails that chatter when the wind blows. Continue until you are no longer outside the moment, no longer anxious, no longer hopeful.

Evidence: Prayer

These are the days of thunder, of quivering, rain-soaked leaves, of things starting out one way and ending another. The air is so humid now it feels like I am drinking water as I breathe, my skin slick, my feet skimming the gravel. I am running hard and I feel like I am flying until I see it out of the corner of my eye, just, and my muscles contract, gravity pulling at my shinbones.

I stop and loop back.

At the side of the road, a hermit thrush with its neck in the pebbles, the tall roadside grasses bending down, shade dappling its feathers. Its eyes are closed, two curved gray marks on the white down of its head, its life a parenthesis between them.

I squat, my hips flexible and loose from running hard in the heat, my knees up by my cheeks, and with a single finger I touch the bird's flecked breast. It is already stiff, its claws drawn up, wings folded close. Its neck is slightly askew, revealing how it might have died: a sudden thud of softly feathered bones and flesh against a windshield, perhaps. A pickup truck, maybe, the farmer's son driving fast, gravel spitting up behind his tires.

I am panting and the backs of my knees are slippery with sweat, but for a hundred minutes, or maybe only one, I am just here.

I cannot take my eyes off of this bird. I've heard the hermit thrush calling in the woods. Its song makes my heart tremble though I can't say why, and now its slender throat rests among the bits of gravel that are also beautiful when I look, shards of quartz scattered among small rocks the color of river sand. I swallow hard and taste salt on my upper lip. Then I stand clumsily and begin to move again, this time toward home.

As I run, I notice the way things are decaying everywhere. Clover cut by the mower's blade, each trio of leaves wilted in the heat, scraggly and drying to a paler green. The sleek shimmering S of a grass snake, pressed flat into the drying mud, its scales like scalloped plates, the road stained dark with its sticky blood. A cluster of brittle leaves where a twig is ripped partway from a sassafras branch, each dead leaf curling inward like a frail fist. And I can feel the way these things are evidence, just as running is evidence.

This is all I need to remember: There is something fragile and breathtaking in me, like a field of irises; something unstoppable, like the innate instinct that sends salmon upstream through rapids and turbines, following the scent of sweet water. Something tremulous, like the song of the thrush, that tells me this life is meant to be lived ardently, not merely spent. Life is abundant and impermanent. It bursts forth, ripens, and then becomes just as quickly another thing. Leaf to soil. Breath to song. Bone to spirit. Nature claims us, holds us, remakes us again and again.

I stop running when I reach the driveway and feel the way my legs are limber, my fingers effortlessly reaching my toes when I bend down. I stretch a bit before walking back to the house, my breath still coming quickly. On the way I duck into the coop to collect the eggs, and find the air astir with the frantic fluttering of a small finch that has gotten caught between the window and the wire-mesh screen. I see it dart in ahead of me out of the corner of my eye, a small figment of shadow and air. It's what they do all day, flitting in and out to feast on the cracked corn we feed the hens, but my arrival has sent this one fluttering in a panic.

I stop where I am and wait for it to still.

The air is pungent and intense with the scent of ammonia and straw, and dust motes fall in golden angles toward the floor. Eventually, when the bird quiets and my breath grows steady, I go to it, reaching a slender wrist down between the glass and screen, my fingers spread wide. It tries to fly.

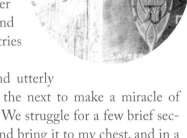

It spreads its wings, brown and utterly perfect, each feather layered upon the next to make a miracle of flight, and tries to escape my hand. We struggle for a few brief seconds. Then I clutch it in my palm and bring it to my chest, and in a single quick gesture carry it to the door and let it go.

Go outside and find a spot where you can touch the ground. Sit on a hillside, maybe, looking south. Listen to the way the air hums with insects. The light will be hazy and golden. Lie back. Turn your face up to the sky and feel the way the earth claims the weight of your body.

Throw your arms wide, your palms open, and let this be the way that you pray.

Let your prayer be about the glory of new grass blades. Let it be about the secretive way the bees make honey in their hive, gathering pollen from a thousand flowers. Let it be about the way things begin, and begin again—you and the grass and the honeybees and the sky.

Field Notes:
PRAYER

prayer |prer|(n.):
a solemn entreaty or expression of thanks.

Lie still until your mind slips to somewhere just before dreaming. Lie with your eyes closed and trace the mottled heat map of red and cobalt that the sun makes on the inside of your lids. Lie still until you remember what you are made of; until your limbs become the grassy hill; your vertebrae, pebbles; your fingers, saplings. Linger for as long as necessary to believe this evidence.

Linger until you can feel the way the sun and the earth and the sky can remake you.

Encountering Possibility:
Prototype

In an attempt to make more space in the tool-shed, my husband has cleared a heap of debris, piling it below the tall pine trees out in front like so many forlorn holiday presents: a shamble of insulation, rusty parts to old tools, broken plastic tubs, a crate of mildewed books, a stack of odd-size boards. He wants to take them all to the dump, but the dump hours are inexplicably inconvenient—between 9:00 a.m. and 4:00 p.m. weekdays, and on Saturdays between 10:00 a.m. and 1:00 p.m.—and we've never managed to borrow the neighbor's truck to load everything and go during these times.

And so the rubbish sits, unwanted, growing even more mildewed and derelict as rain falls and heat coaxes insects to crawl into the mushy places and dark corners to metamorphose the way they do, caterpillars becoming moths, larvae becoming beetles and other crawly things.

"We could use these boards for a tree fort," I suggest to Liam, kicking the stack of wood as we stand there in the yard.

A world to be born

I was a free-range West Coast kid with skinned knees and frugal, distracted parents. Inventing something out of almost nothing was the only way that I survived.

My husband grew up on the opposite coast, in a suburban neighborhood in the New Jersey town Einstein once called home. He had skateboards and a pool and Saturday-morning cartoons, and now when he looks at the pile and says, "No way!" with almost comic contempt, it's because he believes the boards are too irregular, not long enough, or too rough hewn or old for such a project.

It's true. The heap is made up of odd-size ends, scraps, leftovers. There's a sheet of plywood with small rectangular cutouts in the corners, maple pieces glued together, a strip of flooring, a piece of particleboard painted white and heavy as stone. To him they're a mess; but to me, they represent possibility.

So later, when Rian wakes up from his nap and Liam begs, "I just want a fort so bad Mama!" I decide to seize the opportunity. I know in a handful of days everything will land in the new constellations of autumn, like jacks tossed with the bounce of a ball: the beginning of school, the start of new routines and adventures yet to be named. There are ripening apples and sunshine and unfinished things everywhere that call for my attention, but today is one of those summer days when my to-do list feels like a feral cat anyway, rubbing at the screen door of my mind again and again, then running when I open it.

So I agree, and then wait as he hunches over his black-and-white Adidas, fingers moving with careful intention to produce two floppy bows, tied all by himself. And then we go out to the garage to collect a hammer, nails, and a saw.

He is already talking nonstop. "How are we going to make it? And where are we going to build the fort—out here?"

"Let's build it wherever you want," I say, grinning. "Let's make it wherever you want to play in it."

"How about right here?" Liam calls, scooting up the hill to his swing that hangs from a spreading hickory at the edge of the upper meadow.

"Sure," I agree, and we fetch the odds and ends of wood from the debris pile with his red wagon. Then we pick out a little triangle of trees and begin hammering whatever wood we've got into place. When the pieces are too short we hammer one onto the next, not worrying about aesthetics, or cross-bracing, or supports (he weighs all of forty pounds soaking wet). Instead, I focus on just building this thing with him right now: a slanting little place of magic, with tilting windows and wobbly steps.

He's grinning wider than he has all summer.

"Let's use this tubing as a doorbell!" he exclaims, holding a piece of ribbed plastic tubing that used to attach to an inflatable mattress pump. It makes a shrill whistling sound when he blows through it, and he says, "When you come up, blow through it, and if I blow back you can come in." His voice is pitched high with enthusiasm and glee.

"This is a boat," he declares next. "A racing boat. And here is a lock, and how do I write 'Do not enter'?"

This is what happens when you take action in the moment— when you dive in with whatever you've got and make the thing you dream. It doesn't have to be good. It doesn't have to be perfect, or even all right; it just has to be the first inkling of something that you want, something that you're willing to put time into, something that coaxes your imagination to take flight.

New ideas always find me this way, ramshackle, delightful, and unexpected. And I am convinced that ideas are everywhere, like wild daisies, there for the picking. We all have access. Anyone can snag the corner of an idea and give it a tug, pulling down from the firmament some fragment of greatness. It's not a lack of ideas that stops us from creating great work; it's that we make too many excuses and lack the courage to dream things real. It's that having the guts to yank an idea out of the ether and toss it into a cycle of rapid prototyping, drafting, and revising requires focus and risk. The creative process is always an encounter with the unknown, and demands a willingness to veer off course and be transformed.

As a rule, my best ideas arrive when it's least possible to capture them. I think of things when I'm in the shower, when the day feels new and blurry with steam and soap, or when I'm driving home from somewhere, and nowhere near a pen. If I'm lucky, I remember a handful of words, or an image that I can return to when I'm ready to do the work of making it real. What matters is taking action: putting words down, spilling ink, pushing paint around on the page, gluing things or ripping them. What counts is committing to the process, in spite of the possibility that the whole thing might end up a terrible failure, a hodgepodge, a mess. And each time I do this, I realize that if I am brave enough—if I persist for long enough, without logic or doubt or distractions—I can create the first hint of something that is authentic and true.

This is the work of following the spark, the glimmer, the transitory whisper of a story, until it takes me to its wild, uncharted source.

There are many days when every part of me actively resists this process. It feels terribly risky to have such flirtations with the universe. I think of one excuse after the other, like a badminton birdie zipping back and forth, in one instant aiming straight and true, in the next caught by an eddying breeze. Then away I go, off track, especially when I'm online, where one thing leads to the next, everything too available, pertinent, immediate, insistent. I bookmark a hundred things to return to that I find to be brilliant or insightful or relevant to my life, yet even as I click BOOKMARK, I recognize the inevitable mathematics of that action in this moment: Twenty-four hours are divided into innumerable slivers, and my attention grows thin. I realize that none of these things will help me to listen *now*, or to grow still.

The sun is shining, and in the garden, worms creep. Without eyes they are attuned only to the deep vibrations of the earth. On a trellis made of branches, the peas need picking, their tattered white blossoms fluttering like prayer flags in the wind. What matters is listening and then making something happen before the idea slips away—before fall turns to snow and there is no time for playing among trees in an off-kilter little perch. What matters is the way my son grins brightly as he picks up each oddly cut board, imagining it as something, then hammering it into place.

The people who get credit for good ideas don't have any more good ideas than anyone else. They're just more willing to be playful, like small children, and to let the materials at hand spark innovation: a ballpoint pen and scraps of paper; gel medium and images ripped from magazines; a stick to scrawl marks with on a dirt road; or whatever is handy to record the sound and color of an idea when it lands. They understand that ideas show up in a haphazard heap, not as a fully formed *Eureka!*, and they aren't afraid if things start out a mess (and stay that way for a long time). They're in it for the process, and are willing to put everything on the line again and again, prototyping an idea until it becomes real.

Eventually I find a spot in the shade on the crumbling stone wall that once marked the boundary between the field and the woods, and just watch as Liam plays, using everything at hand: the acorns underfoot, the hip-high grass in the field, bark, thread, wire, screws, rocks. Each material offers a spark, a connection, an invitation. Inevitably, the acorns become projectiles; then the tallest grass stalks become antennas for the radio he makes from a bit of bark with a few wooden knobs wired to it. He knows intuitively what I must relearn again and again—that without imagination and the impetus to act, even a very good idea is simply the product of synapse activity, the gesture of the mind going through the motions of thought. What makes an idea great is committing to it. It's leaping toward a half-formed, blurry thing. It's catching a glimpse of a spark, a wild daisy of an idea, and then taking action, playfully, eagerly, immediately.

This is how remarkable things manifest: with playful attention; with a willingness to make things imperfectly real. You have to be willing to have things fail, and to learn from the failures. Think *error recovery* instead of *failure avoidance*. Think with daring. Then act, right now.

My son gets this intuitively. He doesn't hesitate at the edge of a sandbox, or beside a puddle. He jumps in. He is always putting things together in unexpected ways, always pretending, exploring, imagining. He has no concern at all for right angles or precision. All he cares about is the adventure of making, the materials at hand, and the possibilities that unfold.

This is a dare: Whatever dream or plan or great idea you've had in the back of your mind, take some action toward achieving it, right now.

Here are the rules: Suspend disbelief, judgment, and any other mental models that exist for the sole purpose of imposing logic on a situation. Submerse yourself in observation. Acknowledge the inklings. Then act in an instant. Use whatever is at hand. Move to prototyping before you are even done conceptualizing. Lose yourself entirely in the process. Keep things loose and playful. Persist even when you feel like you have just created something horrible, or insignificant or stupid. Delve further. Say more, make more—hold nothing back.

Then do it all over again.

IBLE

Field Notes:
PROTOTYPE

prototype | ˈprō tə tīp | (v.):
to make a first, or preliminary,
model of something from which
other forms are developed.

Deciding: Timing

I feel it in the pit of my stomach like a collection of pebbles: the significance of deciding something that could change my life. And as I walk out into the meadow, my heart whirs like a swarm of bees. How fragile everything feels now. Dew drenches my feet as my ankles tilt and slant, holding me upright among the wayward thistles and wet clover. I can smell the scent of wild roses, sweet like honey, and as I follow it I can feel the weight of everything I cannot know about the outcome that will occur.

It's big, this decision. It will mean doing everything differently from here on out. It will mean drastically changing course, asking for help, and depending on others. It will mean beginning something I have always wanted to begin, officially, with words attached—*Master of Fine Arts*—and in my in-box, an e-mail with a scholarship offer and a very short acceptance deadline. By the end of tomorrow I'll have to say yes or no.

The whole thing feels implausible. There are heaps of odds stacked against me, and there are a thousand reasons why I should not even attempt it. I am the mother of two young boys. Our income will be scant if we continue to live on one salary for another year. And yet I can feel it—the thing that is wild and unkempt in my heart that persists, that howls to be claimed.

I lie down now on the wet grass beneath the roses and try to simply breathe, but the enormity of the situation lands on me with the same force I felt when I fell from a tree as a child. I remember looking up at the dappled leaves, my mouth gaping like a fish until my breath returned and I could begin to cry. Arrhythmia for ten seconds, maybe twelve, a forced pause, and this is exactly what it feels like now, trying to imagine myself in the future of the decision that I'll make. I've spent many months trying to find the groove where the cartilage of necessity meets the bone of love and dreaming, and I can feel the way I'm on the cusp of that discovery, that answer, right now.

I lie staring up at the leaves and the blue and make imaginary lists of pros and cons. I look hopefully for signs, but the sky is cloudless, and the warm air offers only the buzz of honeybees and the distant drone of traffic, and eventually I get up and walk back to the house and go about my work.

It's in the midst of things, as I start preparing dinner, that I notice the praying mantis out of the corner of my eye. It is crawling, with its awkward stilt legs, up the bright red curve of the pepper mill by the stove.

It is summer and there are insects everywhere, but how did it find its way here, a pale leafy green against the red enamel mill we use to crush peppercorns over Manchego and arugula at dinner? I watch it circle the cylinder once, twice, and then I go to it, cup it in my hands, carry it to the screen door, and set it softly on the wide leaves of a hollyhock outside.

And later in the evening, as if to be sure I've understood that I must open the door to this possibility of wildness and longing that the future offers now, a mouse springs the trap under the stove. It is caught by a slender, delicate leg, pink, with the finest silvery hairs. I take it carefully outside and in the middle of the lawn, I unhinge the trap. The mouse falls softly to the grass in the dark, and it's so still that I lean down close to see if it is breathing. The porch light illuminates everything—its minute hairs and transparent ears, and the way we're both breathing quickly. And for a brief hesitation, we stay this way, both looking.

Then it skitters off, leaving me alone in the circle of yellow light on the lawn.

Tomorrow the morning will come. In five years' time, it is likely you will no longer remember the urgency of how these moments of deciding feel. How the weight of this decision feels like encountering the heaviness of your body again after swimming in the ocean for hours, when your legs feel like pillars of sand and your feet keep disappearing beneath you as the tide sucks at your ankles. You will remember this time vaguely, if at all.

Maybe you'll be sitting where you sat when you decided: on a white-cushioned chair, maybe, your feet bare, afternoon light making triangles of shadow on the walls. Or you might remember only that it was simply another beginning. As important and meaningful as the decision is right now, when it comes down to it, it will be just a blip in your large, beautiful life. It will be the work that follows after the decision that will endure.

Knowing this now is important. Let it give you the courage to say what you need to say: yes or no.

Field Notes:
TIMING

timing | 'tim ing| (n.):
the choice, judgment, or control of when something should be done; a particular point or period of time when something happens.

Whatever you decide will be the right
choice; whatever path you choose will be
another beginning.

Another opportunity to offer something
wild and truthful and fragile to the world.

III/26/13 A 1/141/66

Taking Flight: Tyro

I am making espresso when I see it out of the corner of my eye. A sudden swoop, a fluttering movement in the leaves of the lilac tree. When I look more closely I see there is a nest hidden among the branches and dappled shade, and the mother has just arrived to feed her fledglings. I thumb through the field guide I keep on a ledge by the dining-room windows until I find her gold-tipped tail and tawny breast: a cedar waxwing.

When I carry my cup to the window to watch, she becomes completely still, and so do the four babies, until I become the window, the stillness of the wall. Then she lifts off in rapid flight and returns, leaves and returns again, swooping in among the twigs and dark green leaves to feed her scraggly brood that's already outgrowing its small nest. I watch in wonderment at what they will achieve: flight, soon, from the edge of the nest.

• • •

When I was nine I snuck an umbrella out to recess in the sleeve of my sweatshirt on a windy day. The boys did the same with theirs. We were counting on the fact that the soccer game happening in the middle of the field would distract the teachers, and we ran as fast as we could to the toolshed at the edge of the playground. The Santa Ana winds were blowing. We'd been planning this stunt for weeks.

I remember the way the leaves on the apricot trees by the fence were bent in the wind as we climbed up the back of the shed and onto the roof. Then, we stood with our sneakers in a row at the edge. Me, and the boys I always ran with, the wind gusting so hard our

sweatshirts billowed. We were possibly too old to believe in such things, but I remember feeling so light and small, standing there like that, that it seemed entirely possible we'd just lift off.

On the count of three we jumped, our umbrellas flung open above us.

I remember feeling the wind catch then, for a brief interlude, before it snapped the metal spokes of the umbrella inside out. A second, or maybe two, and in that time I was flying. When I hit the ground I wasn't hurt—or if I was, I don't remember. All I remember is jostling for my place at the back of the shed again, for two more seconds of flight.

There is a part of me that keeps wanting risk to feel as easy and graceful as it did when I was small; when I didn't hesitate at the possibility of failure, and there was less to fear with falling. Less distance, weight, impact, consequence. Now there is so much more to lose, and to be gained. An MFA, and a future of full-time creative work. The possibility of being greater than I have ever dared; of becoming something I have never been. And this: I might come up short, fail utterly, look like a fool. In fact, it is almost certain I will make hundreds of mistakes I can't even imagine.

But this isn't about failure avoidance.

• • •

The fledglings' beaks are still large and yellow, like caricatures of the birds they will become, but already they have juvenile feathers, and soon, their nest of twigs and thistledown and bits of blue ribbon in the lilac tree will no longer be enough. The dappled shade of farther branches will beckon, and a day will arrive when they will make a willing leap into the empty air—despite never having flown before. They know innately that lifting off is everything. Attempting is everything.

Falling and flying are the inextricable facets of becoming. We fall in love. We fall because there is no other word for what we do when we are trying to fly.

• • •

The nightly news is dire. There is oil in the Gulf, icebergs shearing off, threats real and perceived. There is the Internet, the wildfire spread of information, the possibility of anything shared in a rush, 140 characters at a time. There are endless devastating facts: terrorists, dying bees, terminator genes that modify the plants we grow and eat, the finiteness of drinking water, the potential of cancer, malaria, warfare, error, mishap.

Yet the truth is, most of the fears that really stop us from taking the risks that matter in our lives are imagined, flighty things spawned by our inability to be right here, and to feel the way the moment offers abundance. The songbirds know how to do this. They take flight effortlessly and navigate the arc of sky in spite of wind or storm. They navigate with certainty, even as the landscape below them is uncharted, toward the fern-filled woods of their migratory home, always following the song lines of their future selves.

I discovered the other day that the Latin root for the word *amateur* means "to love," and it explains exactly the way I feel now, new at everything: vulnerable and awkward, with an eager heart.

amateur (n.): somebody who does something for pleasure; somebody who loves something; an unskilled person.

I also found that the word *happy* comes from the same root as *to happen*. In other words, to experience happiness means to participate wholly in whatever is happening right now. This is the secret: Being at the heart of the moment isn't about being small at all, though many times it comes down to taking note of the smallest of things.

Doing the day is not enough. Living to work is not enough. Rushing always, consuming always, is not enough.

Yet this is the way most of us live our lives. We reach adulthood and then gradually slip toward a kind of circling stasis. Responsibilities press in: mortgages and children, and the careers we have to sustain them. Without intending to, we let our most urgent, wild, creative selves grow quiet under layers of accumulated stress and distraction. And our fear of being new at something—of starting out and maybe failing—is what keeps us from risking all that we are, to become all that we are meant to become.

Yet everything is a risk. Loving. Trying to put down roots. Giving birth. Going out the front door. Taking action on behalf of your creative life. There is always the chance of failure, a shake-up, a mistake, a fight or accident or empty bank account, a collision, a splinter under a fingernail, a fall. This, then, is the challenge: to aim straight for the heat at the center of newness, and let risk bring what it may—wild creativity, curiosity, and abundance, or anxiety, error, and self-doubt.

Either way, the possibility is here, right now: to be great, to make a spark, to start something, to be made new.

• • •

I watch all week, hopeful that I'll be home on the day the fledglings first take flight. And when they do, the sky is full of clouds and rain and thunder passing through, and I think there is no way they'll risk so much, but when I look, the nest is empty. I stand at the window, sad that I've missed them, until I see all four, flitting between the smallest branches of the adjacent tree. There, among the dripping leaves, the distance is calculable—only a few wing-flaps from branch to branch—and this is what they are doing now, flying back and forth among the twigs, high and low. I bring my laptop to the dining-room table so that I can watch them as I work. Mostly I watch.

All morning they flutter, sometimes faltering awkwardly as they land. They preen, then fly again and again, each time farther. The storm blows through. The sky clears. And one by one they leave the shelter of the tree, taking flight into the blue.

• • •

There is no other way to begin, than to begin. Becoming who you are meant to be always requires this: starting, and starting again, for this is the only way to encounter possibility as it unfolds. It's the act of brushing up against the unknown that ignites will and chance and potential.

This is the secret: Being at the heart of the moment isn't about being small at all, though many times it comes down to taking note of the smallest of things. Commitment and passion and certainty emerge in the present tense when you arrive and take note: of the white cat crossing the bridge with a black mouse in its mouth; the red cows chest-deep in clover; the hills turning to flame with fall. Confidence emerges from being right here, through the repeated practice of showing up and taking note. This is a challenge: to notice, to sink deeply into the raw edges, and to find out where the fabric of your life is spun.

These moments are yours. What do they tell you? What are the tracks, the characteristics and traits; what are the calls? This is the work of finding yourself in the moments that matter in your life; of taking hold of them, and identifying them, so that through this activity, you can find sustenance and wonder in your life, even as it is uncertain, or frightening, or limited by circumstance.

Try this: Take the questions on the next page and sit with them. Write about whatever arises. Dig. Be honest, and put words to everything that arises. Find some quiet and a good notebook and pen and begin. Answer each question, one after the other, without hesitation, without analysis. Let this be a way to arrive in the present tense of your heart. Maybe try doing this every day for a week, and watch how your responses change over time.

Field Notes:
TYRO

tyro | ˈtī rō | (n.):
a beginner in learning anything; novice.

This is a springboard, a possibility, a promise: Imagination is more than a state of mind. It's a state of becoming.

What shapes you?

What do you long for?

What can you make happen?

What is within your power right now, right here in these moments?

Acknowledgments

This book would not exist without my editor, Mary Norris, who believed in this project from the start, and without Nikki Hardin, who discovered it on Kickstarter.

It also would not exist without the support of my in-laws, Vincent and Sandra Sbarro, who offered countless hours of child care, meals, and open arms. I am deeply grateful to them both, and to my husband, Todd, for his unswerving belief in my ability, and his willingness to edit drafts in the eleventh hour and grow with me always.

I am also grateful to Willow Mata for being my book midwife. Her thoughtful reading of the work as it was in progress, and her reminders that I could do it when the task seemed daunting, made all the difference. Susan O'Kane, Kait Stokes, Hilary Hess, Kevin Murakami, and Jeremy Smith each also helped me to remember what I was capable of when I needed to hear it most.

Without my sisters and my mother, I would be far less brave. Without Pam Houston and the encouragement of the PAMFAS, I wouldn't have known how to begin.

And finally, I want to thank all of my Kickstarter backers for their generosity and support, particularly Ken Mumma, Dawn Gehring, Rick Langbecker, Laura Brines, Beth Nicholls, Kim Hadley, Betsy Jaeger, Shona Cole, Kristina Roth, Katie Sommerfeld, Honey Trabitz, Peggy Sarjeant, Paul Frank, Annie Cowan, Sandy Copp, Mary Kate Walker, Karen Stewart, Lisa D'Ambrosio, Richard Story, Cara Dobrev, Tara Bradford, Cheryl Unruh, Steph Tigert, Pixie Campbell, Dominique Ridley, Meg Hatton, Elizabeth Slaughter-Ek, Juan Jose Mata, Hashi Meltzer, Nan Perrott, and Mark Mahle.

About the Author

Christina Rosalie is a writer and mixed-media artist whose award-winning work has been featured in print and online. She is also an adventurer, four-leaf clover finder, autodidact, and optimist, with a tendency to forget things on the roof of her car and a knack for getting paint on her jeans. Christina has an MFA in emergent media, from Champlain College and lives with her family in northern Vermont. Visit her at christinarosalie.com.